GUITAR
FOR EVERYONE

KNACK

GUITAR
FOR EVERYONE

A Step-by-Step Guide to Notes, Chords, and Playing Basics

DICK WEISSMAN

Photographs by Julie Keefe
Photo editor John Klicker

Guilford, Connecticut
An imprint of Globe Pequot Press

KNACK®
MAKE IT EASY

Editor: Keith Wallman
Development Editors: Imee Curiel, Katie Benoit
Cover Design: Paul Beatrice, Bret Kerr
Text Design: Paul Beatrice
Layout: Kevin Mak
Cover photos © shutterstock; back cover photo by Julie Keefe
All interior photos by Julie Keefe

Library of Congress Cataloging-in-Publication Data is available on file.

ISBN 978-1-59921-511-2

The following manufacturers/names appearing in *Knack Guitar for Everyone* with CD are trademarks:
Daisy Rock, Euphanon, Gibson LS, Gore-Tex, Harmony, Kyser, Larson Brothers, Martin, Maurer, Prairie State, Stahl, Vega, Washington Guitar Company

Printed in China

10 9 8 7 6 5 4 3 2 1

This book is dedicated to all of the aspiring guitar players out there. There are so many styles of guitar and so many fine players that it's easy to get discouraged. Remember that if you try to practice on a regular basis, you can do it.

Acknowledgments

Special thanks are due to Imee Curiel, Maureen Graney, Katie Benoit, and Keith Wallman for guiding me through the Knack process. Thanks also go to Richard Colombo, Dan McIlhenny, and John Sabastinas at Artichoke Music; Dan Rhiger at Medicine Whistle Studios, who recorded the accompanying audio tracks; Terry Prohaska, who translated the music to Finale; and to our fine photographer Julie Keefe and photo editor John Klicker.

CONTENTS

INTRODUCTION

The guitar is the world's most popular instrument. It is found in its familiar six-string form in Africa, Asia, Europe, and in North and South America. The instrument that most people are familiar with has six strings and metal bars called frets that run the length of the fingerboard. In many parts of the world people play such instruments as ouds, banjos, or mandolins, that are like members of the guitar's extended family. Some of these instruments have different numbers of strings, some lack frets, and some have shapes that are quite different from the guitar.

The origins of the guitar go back to 2000 B.C. to a five-string Assyrian instrument. Other guitar-like instruments appear in Egyptian cave paintings dated to around 1300 B.C. The Greek *kithara* was a harp-like instrument held in the player's lap, and supposedly the Romans spread the lyre through the Roman Empire. Another relative of the guitar is the *rebab*, a Persian instrument that dates to the tenth century and is still played in Iran and other Asian countries today.

Some combination of the kithara and the Arabic lute brought the guitar to Spain, where it began to assume the shape that we know today. It wasn't a simple process, though. The immediate ancestors of the guitar often had four strings, and later the strings became doubled, as in the construction of the mandolin. So the four-string guitar really had eight strings, and they were played as four double strings. In other words, the strings were in pairs, with the two strings in each pair positioned quite close to one another. A similar arrangement is found on the contemporary 12-string guitar (six pairs) or the mandolin (four pairs).

During the course of its evolution, the guitar had to defeat some competitors to become the instrument that we know today. In the early 1600s the round-backed lute, often with multiple strings, was even more popular than the guitar, especially at the English court. Some of these instruments even had triple sets of strings. By that period, most guitars had gone from four strings to five strings.

The lute was somewhat difficult to master due to its large number of strings, and the guitar achieved a broader base of popularity. Eventually the lute and its cousin the *vihuela*

became virtually extinct, and the guitar became popular throughout Europe. By 1800 the lowest string was added to the guitar, and from that point forward the six-string guitar became the standard model favored by most guitarists.

Over the years the bracing patterns used for the guitar, the shape of the guitar's sound hole, the types of strings used on the various instruments, and amplification have created many changes in the way the guitar sounds, and in the techniques used to play it. The original gut strings, made from sheepgut, were replaced by nylon strings after World War II. Around 1880 steel-string guitars were made by Orville Gibson, among others, and they replaced their nylon-string brothers for players in the folk, country, and blues genres. Pioneer guitar and mandolin designer Lloyd Loar introduced guitars with f holes, instead of round holes. These were holes shaped like violin holes used in jazz guitars. The Gibson L5, in particular, was the favorite axe of many of the early jazz players.

By the mid-1930s electric guitars were introduced into the world of the guitar. Prior to the invention of the pure electric instrument, the same Lloyd Loar had experimented with putting pickups on f-hole guitars. Rickenbacker made the first electric guitars, which were lap steel instruments rather than typical guitars, but by 1936 Gibson had introduced pickups as standard fare on some of its f-hole models.

Part of the evolution of the guitar has come about because of the work of specific musicians whose mastery of the instrument has brought innovations in both playing techniques and in the technology used by luthiers and guitar manufacturers. Although there have been many fine guitarists before and after him, Andres Segovia is considered

the founding father of classical guitar as we know it today. Through his many public appearances, recordings, publications, and master classes, Segovia brought the classical guitar from obscurity into its current role as an instrument used for solo recitals, chamber music, and orchestral works.

Jazz guitar evolved through the early work of pioneering guitarists Eddie Lang and Lonnie Johnson, and through Charlie Christian's brilliant work with Benny Goodman and on early bebop jam sessions. Since those days, such players as Wes Montgomery and Joe Pass have expanded on this legacy.

The history of flamenco, Spanish gypsy guitar, dates from such early masters as Ramón Montoya to the fiery playing of Paco de Lucía. Rock and roll had its own set of monster players, with Jimi Hendrix perhaps being the most innovative and fiery player of a line that includes Jeff Beck, Jimmy Page, Eddie Van Halen, and many, many others. Acoustic folk and country guitar has showcased the talents of Doc Watson, Mississippi John Hurt, John Fahey, Tony Rice, and Leo Kottke, and the great blues guitarists Charlie Patton, Blind Blake, Robert Johnson, B. B. King, and Buddy Guy are among those whose music has changed the playing techniques used in this idiom.

As the phonograph, the radio, and the iPod have spread throughout the world, we now have guitarists active in every conceivable part of our planet. Guitarists in Vietnam and India have experimented with removing the frets from their guitars, enabling them to play notes that utilize the scales that are common to their traditional music. There are several generations of guitarists all over Africa who have played both electric and acoustic guitar not only in their own countries, but in worldwide tours. Such American guitarists as Bob Brozman, Ry Cooder, Henry Kaiser, David Lindley and Taj Mahal have toured throughout the world, and played with musicians from virtually everywhere.

Some musicians have chosen to play the 12-string guitar, in the jazz world players have added a seventh, lower bass string to the instrument that enable players to play additional bass lines, and several classical players are playing guitars with ten strings, in a sense returning the instrument to where it was before luthiers and players settled on the six-string format that most of them still use today.

The purpose of this book is to introduce you to the guitar. The accompanying audio tracks (www.knackbooks.com/guitar) will enable you to hear all of the musical examples that are printed in the book. The guitar can be an occasional fun pastime, or a lifetime pursuit. Whichever one it is for you, it is our intention to help you enjoy it.

By using this book you can started sampling the varied menu of guitar styles. What wonderful jazz players like Jim Hall or Pat Metheny, rock guitarists like Eddie Van Halen or Slash, or the many fine flamenco, blues, classical, or folk players have in common is that they all start by mastering basic guitar chords and by learning how to coordinate their left and right hands.

This book will provide you with the basic tools that will enable you to choose what style of guitar is the one that

you will concentrate on as you develop some facility on the instrument. The guitar is a very versatile instrument, and ultimately your choice of musical style will be limited only by your imagination.

In this book we will be dealing with the basics—how to find a guitar, how to hold it, and how to develop some simple left- and right-hand techniques that will provide you with years of fun. After you master the basics, we will lead you on an exploration of a few techniques that will provide the building blocks for those years of fun that await you. Let's get started!

BASIC GUITARS
This section will introduce you to the many varieties of guitars

A well-stocked music store will carry a wide variety of guitars. The kind of guitar that you want to purchase (or rent) is largely dependent upon the sort of music that you prefer to play. First you need to decide whether you want to play an electric or an acoustic guitar. If your budget is an important factor, then the decision is a simple one. Electric guitars require the use of an amplifier, which represents an additional expense.

If you have chosen to start on an acoustic guitar, you have another choice to make. Do you wish to play a nylon-string guitar or a steel-string guitar? This choice is governed by two factors: the sort of music that you want to play, and the strength of your left hand. Nylon-string guitars do not require as much left-hand pressure as steel-string guitars. Price is not really a factor here, because in both categories, reasonably

Nylon-string Guitar

- Nylon-string guitars have wide necks. If you have small hands, you may find playing a wide neck to be awkward.

- Nylon-string guitars are almost always played with the right-hand fingers, without the use of picks.

- Nylon-string guitars are ideally suited for playing classical and flamenco music. There are also a number of guitarists who play jazz and bossa nova on nylon-string guitars.

- Music stores tend to carry fewer nylon-string guitars than steel-string models.

Steel-string Guitar

- The steel string guitar has a narrower neck than its nylon-string cousin.

- In order to play the steel-string guitar, you need to apply more pressure, especially with your left hand.

- Steel-string guitars are ideally suited for playing

blues, country, folk, and rock music.

- Steel-string guitars are the most popular kind of guitars available, and are found in almost every music store.

well-made good-sounding guitars are available for $200 or less.

If you are not sure what you want, and you haven't played before, take along a friend or have the salesman play both sorts of guitars for you, so that you can hear the differences between the nylon- and steel-string instruments. Be sure that you buy your guitar at a store that can repair it. Otherwise you're in for a number of 1-800 calls, and some shipping hassles.

ZOOM

Nylon-string guitars are better for playing soft ballads or classical guitar music. Steel-string guitars are an essential tool if you are playing rock or blues music. Nylon-string guitars are virtually never played with a flat pick or fingerpicks, while steel-string instruments can be played with or without fingerpicks or flat picks.

Guitar with Cutaway Neck

- Cutaway guitars have the body of the instrument cut away so that the guitarist can access high notes.

- The cutaway guitar makes it easy to play notes high on the guitar neck.

- Cutaway guitars are popular with jazz and rock guitar players. Classical guitarists do not use cutaway models.

- Cutaway guitars are most often found in large music stores.

Cowboy Guitar

- Cowboy guitars are generally used more for decoration than for actual playing.

- Some music stores have displays of dozens of cowboy guitars. Cowboy guitars have decorative western motifs.

- Recently the Martin company has made some cowboy guitars for fans of Americana.

- If western movies ever come back, you can be sure there will be a great demand for these instruments.

1

ACOUSTIC GUITARS

Acoustic guitars are wonderful for solo playing, and can also be used in small bands

There are dozens of excellent acoustic guitars. They come in different body sizes, so whether you are tall or small, or have large or small hands, you should be able to find a guitar suitable for your body type. There is even a guitar company called Daisy Rock that makes guitars designed for women to play.

Twelve-string guitars are tuned just like the six-string models, except that three of the sets of strings are tuned an octave apart. The 12-string requires considerable pressure in the left hand, and we don't recommend it for beginners.

F-hole guitars are used in playing jazz rhythm guitar. They have a more contained sound, rather than featuring the

12-string Guitar

- Leadbelly was known as the king of the 12-string guitar. He died in 1949.

- Twelve-string guitars require tremendous pressure in the left hand in order to finger chords.

- The Mexican 12-string guitar is known as the *bajo*

sexto. It is commonly used in *norteno*, the music of southern Texas and northern Mexico.

- During the 1960s, the 12-string was featured in folk-rock music. The Byrds popularized the electric 12-string guitar.

Guitar with F Holes

- F-hole guitars have a clipped, contained sound that works especially well in jazz guitar.

- Early electric guitars were f-hole guitars with pickups mounted on the face of the guitar.

- In the 1920s, f-hole guitars began to replace the banjo in the rhythm sections of jazz combos.

- Modern handmade f-hole guitars are very expensive, and a bit hard to find.

sounds of the open strings ringing. Jazz rhythm guitar is often played with a medium or large band, and the more subdued sound blends in with these ensembles more effectively.

The *requinto* is a small-bodied nylon-string guitar that is tuned higher than the usual guitar. In Latin-American guitar styles the requinto is often used for playing lead parts, with a larger-bodied guitar playing rhythm.

Requinto

- Requintos are small-bodied guitars that are tuned to a higher pitch than normal guitars.

- In Mexican music requintos typically play lead guitar, while a normal-sized acoustic guitar plays the rhythm.

- If you want to find a requinto, it is best to go to a store that specializes in Mexican musical instruments.

Lap Steel

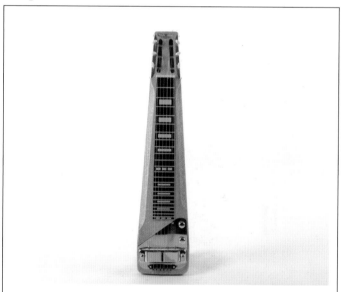

- Lap steel guitars are used in country and western music.

- Bluegrass musicians use an acoustic version of the lap steel, called a dobro.

- In western music, the pedal steel guitar, a much larger and more complex instrument, is used instead of the lap steel.

3

ELECTRIC & MISCELLANEOUS GUITARS
This section introduces a few of the many other varieties of guitars

The electric solid-body guitar is ideally suited for playing rock and roll. This instrument is almost invariably played with a flat pick used by the right hand, rather than the right-hand fingers. It is capable of quite a few sound variations, either by increasing or decreasing the amount of treble or bass sounds on the guitar's pickups, or by adjusting the sounds offered by the guitar amplifier.

Slide guitar involves the use of a device that is usually worn on the left-hand pinky or ring finger. Many slide guitarists play in tunings that are different from normal guitar tunings.

The dobro is an instrument that has a resonator, and is played flat. Instead of using the left hand to finger chords, the dobro is played with a steel bar played by the left hand. This instrument is often used in bluegrass bands.

Electric Solid-body Guitar, Ideal for Rock and Roll

- Electric guitars are ideally suited for playing rock and roll. It's hard to imagine many rock tunes without the presence of an electric guitar.

- Electric guitars require the player to use an amplifier.

- In addition to its role in rock and roll, the great majority of jazz guitarists use electric guitars.

- Electric guitars are readily available. They vary widely in price, and many players prize older instruments.

Guitar with a Steel Resonator Body

- Slide guitars are wonderful instruments for playing Delta blues.

- During the 1930s, resonator guitars were in wide use, because they were much louder than normal acoustic instruments.

- Currently several companies are making resonator guitars that are ideal for slide playing, after a long period when only used instruments were available.

- Slide guitar technique is a unique guitar style.

A tenor guitar has only four strings. It is used as a rhythm guitar, usually along with a six-string guitar playing lead lines. The Kingston Trio featured a tenor guitar in its music, and it is also sometimes used by swing guitarists.

ZOOM

The slide guitar is frequently used in modern blues and rock and roll recordings. Slide guitar can be played on an acoustic guitar or an electric instrument. The sound of the slide is evocative of blues history and the roots of guitar as played in the Mississippi Delta by such artists as Robert Johnson. Ry Cooder and Eric Clapton are among the modern masters of slide technique.

Dobro—Played with Steel Bar in the LH

- The dobro is played with a steel bar held in the left hand.

- The dobro is often used in bluegrass music.

- The dobro is coming into its own, because of such contemporary virtuosos as Jerry Douglas.

- The dobro doesn't have frets.

Ukulele

- The ukulele is a cousin of the tenor guitar.

- Although it was originally used in Hawaiian music, today there are many versatile players.

- There are also modified ukes that have six strings instead of four strings. Often the uke plays with guitar.

- Such fine players as Lyle Ritz are even playing jazz uke. Others are even adapting classical music for the uke. The uke is no longer a novelty instrument.

VINTAGE & TRAVEL GUITARS

Vintage guitars are highly sought after by collectors, while travel guitars are a portable alternative

Vintage guitars are guitars that have been in use for some years. Many artists prize guitars made in particular time periods. For example, Martin guitars stopped using Brazilian rosewood after 1968, and any Martin instruments made before that time are considered particularly valuable. Any Gibson guitar that carries the signature of the legendary Lloyd Loar is extremely sought after by collectors.

During the 1920s and 1930s, there were a number of fine American guitar makers, such as the Larsen Brothers and the Washburn Guitar Company, and these instruments are also quite expensive and sought after by professionals and guitar collectors.

KNACK GUITAR FOR EVERYONE

1913 Vega Guitar

Guitar Made in the 1970s by Michael Gurian

- Vintage guitars are extremely collectible, and many players are willing to pay thousands of dollars for certain models.

- Don't buy a vintage guitar unless you have someone check out its condition. Sometimes the repair costs can be hundreds of dollars,

  and collectors prefer instruments that have all of the original parts, such as tuning gears or the bridge.

- It is possible to find out the value of a vintage guitar through guitar bluebooks.

- You can search for vintage guitars at flea markets, antique shops, and pawnshops.

- Guitar bluebooks tell you how to determine a guitar's exact age by using the serial numbers found inside the instrument.

- Magazines such as *Vintage Guitar* discuss and advertise vintage instruments.

Many of the guitar manufacturers of this earlier era marketed their instruments under various names for certain retail stores or mail-order catalogs. For example, Larsen Brothers instruments were marketed under the names Euphonon, Maurer, Prairie State, and Stahl.

Travel guitars are designed to be extremely portable. Many of them fit in a backpack and can be brought on camping trips or easily carried on an airplane. The earliest travel guitars were inexpensive and didn't sound especially good, but some of the instruments of today are well-made.

MAKE IT EASY

Many traveling musicians look for vintage instruments. There are many tales of rare instruments tracked down at pawnshops, antique stores, or flea markets. Because many of these instruments have eventually self-destructed, and because so many people are seeking them, it has become more difficult to find vintage instruments. Trade collectors and store owners look for these sought-after antiques at annual guitar shows.

Small-size Guitar Ideal for Traveling

- Travel guitars are smaller and lighter than normal instruments.

- It takes a bit of time to get used to playing travel guitars because their body size is smaller than the size of the average guitar.

- The first travel guitars were cheap and not well-constructed, but nowadays it is possible to spend quite a bit of money on a quality travel instrument.

Flamenco Guitar, Made of Cypress Wood

- Flamenco guitar is the music of the Spanish gypsies. It was originally intended to accompany singing and dancing, but now solo flamenco guitar is quite common.

- The younger generation of Spanish flamenco players is quite adventurous, integrat-

- ing jazz and even rock techniques with gypsy guitar.

- Authentic flamenco guitars use violin tuning pegs. These are difficult to manipulate, until you get used to them.

- You probably will need to find a guitar specialty shop to get a flamenco guitar.

IMPORTANT GUITAR PARTS

Knowing the parts of the guitar will enable you to choose a good instrument

It is important to know the various parts of the guitar in order to diagnose any problems that require repair. The guitar neck comes in various widths, and it is vital that you choose a guitar that is appropriate for the size of your hand. If the guitar is too wide for the size of your hand, your left hand can become quite sore, and you will have trouble fingering the chords. If

the guitar is too narrow, you will have trouble fingering the chords because your fingers will overlap one another.

The tuning gears often differentiate a workable guitar from one that will cause you many headaches. You should be able to turn the gears without exerting a huge amount of effort, and the gears should not slip. If they do slip, you will spend

Neck of Guitar

- The width of a guitar's neck will dictate what sort of guitar you want to purchase. A wide neck is not practical for someone with particularly small hands.

- The width of the neck and the body can make a guitar difficult for an aspiring

player, if they don't suit his or her body size.

- When checking a guitar neck, if the frets feel rough rather than smooth, you could be facing a fret job. Replacing frets is an expensive repair that requires the use of a skilled luthier.

Tuning Gears, Used to Tune Strings

- Tuning gears should be easy to turn. If they are not easy to turn, a drop of machine oil on the gears should help. If this doesn't work, the gears need to be replaced.

- If the guitar's strings are slipping, make sure that the tuning gears are tight.

A small screwdriver will do the trick.

- Cheap tuning gears can make a guitar virtually unplayable.

- The highest-quality tuning gears cost over $100 for a set. These gears are intended for professional players.

an inordinate amount of time unsuccessfully attempting to tune your guitar.

Nylon- and steel-string guitars utilize different sorts of mechanisms to keep the strings in place. Nylon-string guitars require you to tie the string to the end of the guitar, looping it through the bridge. Steel-string guitars use strings that have a little ball at the end of the strings. The string is inserted into the guitar saddle, and covered by an end pin. When you tune the guitar, the end pin must be held in place, or it will pop up.

Bridge

- The guitar bridge should be glued securely on the face of the guitar.

- The strings go over the bridge to the end pins.

- If the bridge comes loose and it comes up, it may damage the face of the guitar.

- The strings of the guitar rest on the saddle. On nylon-string guitars they are tied to the bridge; on steel-string instruments the ball is inserted into the guitar, and secured by a pin.

The Nut

- The nut is the ivory piece between the guitar neck and the tuning gears.

- The strings run over the nut, and are then attached to the tuning gears of the guitar.

- It is important that the nut is filed smoothly, or the strings will buzz.

- If the nut is not filed evenly, the action of the guitar will be uneven, causing you to have trouble fingering the chords in the left hand.

HAND SIZE & NYLON-STRING GUITARS
Part of your choice of guitar will be influenced by the size of your hands

The type of guitar that you choose to buy or rent should be based upon your musical taste and also on the size of your hands in particular and your body size in general.

In terms of fitting the size of your hand, nylon-string guitars generally have wide (2¼") necks, although the tremendous demand for guitars has introduced models in the last twenty years that were previously unavailable. Nylon strings are much softer on the hand than steel strings are.

The height of the strings off the fingerboard will determine how much pressure you need to use with your left hand. If the strings are placed high above the fingerboard, you may hurt your hands when you attempt to finger a chord. If the strings are too low, the instrument will rattle and/or buzz. Finger-style players need to have fingernails on their

Average-size Hand

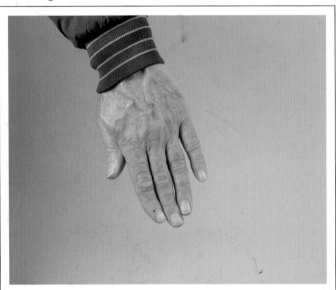

- The size of the left hand is a major factor in determining what size guitar you should purchase.

- Although the size of your hand does affect your playing ability, I have seen some guitarists with very small hands that were very flexible.

- It is also possible to do fingering exercises to develop your ability to make long stretches with your left hand.

Larger-size Hand

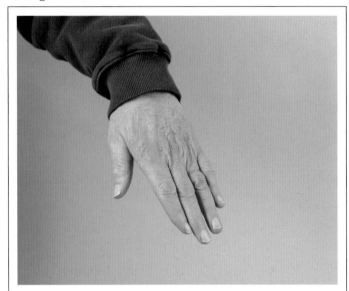

- If you have a large left hand, you need to be sure to buy an instrument that is not too narrow for the size of your fingers.

- Guitarists with exceptionally large hands may have difficulty in fingering intri-cate passages that require control of the hand.

- The position of your left wrist can affect the sound of your playing as much as the actual fingering of the chords.

right hands, but they cannot be *too* long or irregular. You can always tell finger-style guitar players, because they have nails on the right hand, but no nails on the left hand. Pick-style players don't have nails on either hand.

Filing the fingernails is best done with a smooth glass file. When the file has cut the nail to a desirable length, you then take some sort of smooth sandpaper, as shown in the photo on page 19, and make sure that the fingernails are rounded smoothly, with no rough spots to catch the strings.

ZOOM

Filing the fingernails is important, because a smoothly filed fingernail of a little length enables you to produce a good sound, and also to play with volume and power when necessary. Playing loud without fingernails can actually prove to be painful and will also make your hand sore. It's a nuisance, but it will pay off.

Typical Nylon-string Guitar with Wide Neck

- The nylon-string guitar almost always has a wider neck. This can be difficult for someone with a small left hand.

- Classical guitarists, as we will see later in the book, use very specific left-hand fingering techniques.

- There are half-size guitars now available for children who wish to play nylon-string guitars, but whose hands aren't large enough to play the normal-size instruments.

LH Fingering a Chord

- Guitar chords are always fingered just behind the frets, the metal bars that run across the strings on the guitar neck, in the direction of the headstock.

- The exception to this fingering is in slide guitar, where the slide fingers exactly on the frets, rather than behind them.

- We'll have lots more to say about the position of the left hand when it plays chords.

HAND SIZE & STEEL-STRING GUITARS
The steel-string guitar has a narrower neck than its classical compatriot

Steel-string guitars have narrower necks than their nylon-string cousins. The typical steel-string neck is 1³⁄₄" wide, but some steel-strings have necks as wide as 1⁷⁄₈", or as narrow as 1⁵⁄₈". The size of your hand will determine which of these models is best suited to you. If you have a really small hand, a very narrow neck is desirable, because it will enable you to play chords without much difficulty.

Steel-string guitars also come in different body sizes, from the smaller, parlor-size guitars to the dreadnought-style guitars used in bluegrass music. As the number of luthiers and guitar manufacturers has proliferated, the availability of different models has greatly increased.

The steel-string guitar is definitely the instrument of choice for country music, blues, rock, and jazz.

Steel-string Guitar with Wide Neck

Steel-string Guitar, Intermediate-size Neck

- An intermediate-length neck is ideally suited for someone with a normal-size left hand.

- Some steel-string guitars tend to have wider necks than others. Neck widths of 1⁷⁄₈" work well for players with fairly large hands who still want to play steel-string models.

- Even quality players have trouble using guitar necks that are too wide or too narrow for the size of their hands.

- The position of the left wrist will play a powerful role in determining whether you can get a good sound out of your guitar.

- The left thumb often gets in the way of fingering guitar chords. If your thumb feels tense, the sound of the chord is apt to be muffled.

- Be sure that the wood of the guitar feels smooth in your left hand, or you may even have the misfortune to pick up a splinter.

In other styles of music, such as folk music or bossa nova, it is up to the player to decide whether he or she prefers the sound of the steel-string or the nylon-string version.

Advanced players sometimes enjoy the cutaway guitar models, which allow the player easy access to the higher left-hand positions of the guitar. Some steel-strings have twelve-fret necks, while others have fourteen frets. This defines the number of frets available before you reach the body of the guitar. It is a matter of individual taste whether you prefer the twelve- or fourteen-fret models.

One advantage of steel-string guitars over nylon-string models is that steel-string guitars can be played with a flat pick or with plastic or metal fingerpicks. Nylon-string guitars sound awful when played with fingerpicks, and although a few players play nylon-string instruments with a pick, it requires considerable skill to keep the instrument from buzzing or making unpleasant noises.

Narrow-neck Guitar

Fingering a Chord on a Narrow-neck Guitar

- Fingering a narrow neck with the left hand requires that you use your left hand in such a way that it plays only the strings that you are aiming to finger.

- Many players love guitars with narrow necks, and feel that a narrow neck with the height of the strings set low enables them to play very quickly.

- It is possible to make a narrow neck slightly wider by recutting the bridge and the nut. Even small changes in width can be dramatic. It is best to have a qualified luthier do the work.

- With a narrow neck, it can be difficult not to overlap superfluous strings.

- If your left hand becomes tired, it may be because your left wrist is too tense.

- Remember to keep your left thumb behind the neck.

13

THE HEIGHT OF THE STRINGS

The height of the strings will have a major influence on your ease of playing

The height of the strings over the fingerboard plays a key role in determining your ability to play the instrument. To put it another way, high action equals a sore left hand. The action can be influenced by a number of factors. Many mass-produced guitars are built at factories that produce hundreds of guitars a day. If the price tag is low, the chances are that the factory sets up the guitars very quickly, without exercising a great amount of care.

One advantage of buying a guitar from a store that specializes in guitars is that usually the owners of such stores are well aware of the importance of the action, and they will take the time to set up the guitars, rather than simply receiving

Guitar with Strings Too High above the Neck

- When the action is high, your left hand will have difficulty pressing the strings down.

- Some players keep the action fairly high, because it helps to increase the loudness of your playing. However, your left hand should never hurt when you play.

- You have to experiment to come up with the optimal height of the strings. A good repair person can help you, and your teacher should also assist you.

- High action indicates a warped deck.

Guitar with Acceptable Action

- Acceptable action means that your left hand feels fairly comfortable when you finger chords.

- Another factor in determining the action is the thickness of the strings. We will discuss that matter later.

- The action should be low even for easy playing, but high enough to avoid buzzing.

14

them from the factory and placing them on the wall.

Another reason that the guitar's action may be too high is that the neck of the guitar is warped. When the neck is warped, it is impossible to finger the strings without applying tremendous pressure. An opposite problem occurs if the action is set too low. Guitars with very low action are attractive to many players, because it is possible to play such instruments at high rates of speed. However, the price that the player pays is that these guitars often rattle and buzz. This sound is not only annoying to the player, but also unattractive to the listener.

Guitar with Easy Action

- Easy action means that you can play almost without effort in the left hand.

- If the guitar buzzes, the action is too easy.

- Some players are willing to accept the occasional buzz

in exchange for ease of playing.

- The action will feel differently depending on whether you are playing single notes or chords (groups of notes).

Guitar with Unplayable Action

- When the action is high the left hand has trouble pressing on the strings.

- It may even be painful to press the strings when the action is this high.

- The guitar is also apt to play out of tune.

FINGERNAILS

For finger-style players, the length and smoothness of right-hand fingernails is critical

The quality of sound that finger-style players produce largely comes from the impact of the fingernails of the right hand striking the guitar string. If a guitarist plays a steel-string guitar without any fingernails on the right hand, the player will have very sore fingers. For this reason, it is important to maintain fingernails on the right hand. Of course it is possible to play the guitar with a thumb pick and fingerpicks, but the sound is different from the sound of bare fingers. In some ways picks are very efficient, because they enable the player to play at a high level of speed, without ever worrying about breaking fingernails. The downside is that it is difficult to achieve a variety of sound textures with the use of picks.

LH with Fingernails Cut Properly

- If you have no nails on the left hand, you should rarely feel any soreness in that hand.

- Another benefit of cutting your nails short on the left hand is that you will only finger the strings of the chord.

- For the left hand, you can either file your nails, or cut them with a nail clipper.

LH with Fingernails Too Long

- Fingernails on the left hand will interfere with your left-hand fingerings.

- Fingernails can also get caught in the strings. This is annoying, and can even be painful.

- Sometimes nail clippers do not leave the fingernails smooth.

Fingerpicks and thumb picks are available in both steel and plastic, and players will develop their own preferences.

Another advantage of fingerpicks is that it is easy to play loud with them. If the player is in a band, or playing in a venue where there is considerable noise, this can be an advantage.

When the guitarist plays with bare fingers, it is not only the fingernail that strikes the string, but also the fleshy part of the finger just below the nail as well. Some players have trouble maintaining strong fingernails, and some players will have trouble with a specific nail. For example, I have experienced little trouble in maintaining the nails on my index and ring fingers, but my middle fingernail breaks or cracks fairly frequently. It is also possible to strengthen the nails by using gelatin supplements or a nail-hardening beauty product. If a nail breaks in a performing situation, it is possible to use tape to avoid damage to the skin under your nail.

RH with No Fingernails

- If you have no fingernails on the right hand, when you play intensely, it will make tips of your fingers very sore.

- The actual picking part of the right hand is between the fingernails and the flesh of the fingers.

- Some players strum with the thumb. With no nail, this can be painful.

- The lack of nails also affects the volume that you get out of the guitar.

RH with Fingernails Sanded Down

- Smooth fingernails help you to get a good sound.

- Be careful not to leave any sharp edges around the nails.

- The thumbnail should also be smooth.

- The little finger of the right hand is rarely used on the guitar, but you might as well smooth it out too.

FILING THE FINGERNAILS

After using a file on the nails, it is important to smooth the nail with sandpaper

Filing the fingernails is an essential process in developing a good right-hand technique.

First the player should purchase a smooth glass file, not the sort of file that has rough edges. These are not the sort of files found in ordinary drugstores, so it may take a while to find one.

If you can't find one in your town, use a computer search engine and look for a mail order supplier for glass files.

The glass file will take away a fair amount of any excess length of your nail. You will then need to find some very smooth sandpaper to make sure that there are no brittle edges or parts of the nail that can catch the edge of a guitar string.

Various Nail Files

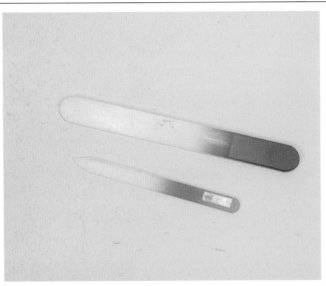

- Ordinary nail files don't work very well for guitar nail filing, because they aren't smooth enough.

- Glass nail files are good for smoothing the nails of the right hand.

- Don't hurry when you are shaping your nails. Take your time, and make sure that the nails are smooth.

Various Thicknesses of Sandpaper

- Sandpaper is used for smoothing RH nails.

- Smaller nail files are quite portable, but they require you to spend more time on your nails.

- Large nail files are less portable, but they work well.

- Medium-size nail files fit comfortably into a guitar case.

Ordinary sandpaper is much too rough for this purpose, so try to find some smooth sandpaper. You might try your local hardware store

As part of your practice routine, you should develop the habit of smoothing your nails before you play. If you allow your fingernails to become too rough, they may very well split, and you will have to erode the entire nail in order to smooth it out. It may take you weeks to get the nail to grow out enough to be useful to your playing.

YELLOW LIGHT

One way to understand the importance of nails is to record your playing at a point when you have nails and at another time when you lack them. You ought to be able to hear a considerable difference in the sound. Ask your teacher or to play the guitar with and without the use of nails, and you'll get the idea. When you go out to see other guitarists, try to get a seat close enough to the stage so that you can observe if they are using fingernails as their playing technique.

Nail File in Use

- File your nails evenly.

- Everyone's nails are a different shape. Be careful to round out edges.

- The smoother the nail, the rounder the tone you will get out of the guitar.

Sandpaper in Use

- Sandpaper is readily available, but you need a smooth grade of sandpaper to round out the nails.

- Remember, this isn't the sort of typical sandpaper product that a hardware store normally has. Be

sure that the sandpaper is smooth, and that you can also buff the nails.

- You may have to find a store that sells classical guitar accessories to find the appropriate sandpaper.

PICKS

There are numerous sizes and shapes of picks available for guitarists nowadays

With the expenditure of very little money, it is possible to purchase a variety of tools that will enhance your ability to play the guitar, and provide you with a good deal of enjoyment. First of all let's discuss flat picks. Flat picks are small picks that are usually held between the thumb and the first finger of the right hand. Picks come in a variety of sizes, shapes, and materials. The most sought-after picks are tortoise-shell picks, but the export of tortoise shell is now banned from the Central American countries that used to supply them. There is something of a black market in illegal tortoise-shell picks, but it is illegal, and the prices are ridiculous.

The obvious question is, what kind of pick is good for you?

Small- and Medium-size Guitar Picks

- Different flat picks fulfill different needs. Most mandolin picks are fairly small, because the instrument has strings set up in pairs.

- Larger guitar picks are more suitable for those who play rhythm guitar.

- It's a great idea to own a number of picks made of different materials, as well as picks of different sizes.

Various-size Picks

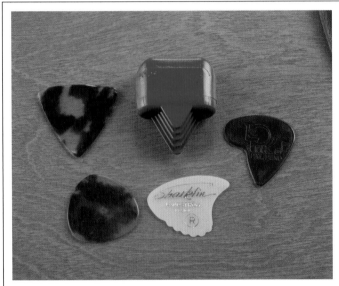

- Some players have trouble with dropping picks. Some manufacturers have developed picks that are designed to help guitarists hold on to them.

- Jazz guitarists are fond of tiny picks that minimize the amount of pick noise made when the string hits the picks.

- There are giant picks, triangular picks, and some that look more like toys than something that you would use on a guitar.

Part of the answer depends upon the style of music that you play. Jazz players tend to favor very small picks, which produce few extraneous sounds. Rhythm rock and roll guitarists tend to like large picks that contribute to the overall volume level that they strive to play. There are plastic tortoise-shell substitutes, odd-shaped picks of all kinds, picks that have a gripping material on the back, so that players have less trouble hanging on to them while playing, and so forth. Because the price of picks is so low, you should indulge yourself and buy a bunch of them.

Often music stores even give them away as a means of promoting the store. After all, with a promotional pick, every time that you play you will see the store's name in your hand.

It is also possible to play using a pick and the middle, ring, and small fingers of the right hand. This is an advanced technique, which we won't discuss here.

Steel and Plastic Fingerpicks

- Metal picks tend to be rather noisy on the guitar. On the other hand, they are capable of plenty of volume.

- Don't wear picks too snugly. If you do, they can actually make your fingers or thumb hurt.

- It's a bit easier to control pick noises with plastic picks than with metal ones.

- Fingerpicks come in different gauges of thickness. Experiment to find the ones you like.

Plastic and Metal Thumb Picks

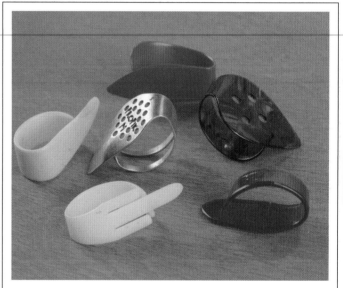

- Thumb picks sometimes have blades on the end of the pick that enable them to function as flat picks, as well as thumb picks.

- The differences between metal and plastic thumb picks are similar to the ones we described above in discussing fingerpicks.

- It is also possible to play using a thumb pick, without fingerpicks.

- Make sure that the thumb pick is a good fit for your thumb.

THUMB PICKS & FINGERPICKS

Finger and thumb picks are worn on the right hand, rather than being held in the hand

Thumb picks are worn on the right thumb. Nowadays there are many sorts of thumb picks available. Some of them even have blades at the edge that enable the player to use the thumb pick as a flat pick when that is desirable. Thumb picks also come in different sizes. You should be sure to buy a thumb pick that fits your thumb, but is not too snug. If the

thumb pick is too tight, it will hurt your thumb, and even your right wrist when you play. Larger thumb picks help to ensure that you will hit the correct string, but they also may produce excessive string noise. The two basic materials available in thumb picks are plastic and metal. Once again it is a matter of taste as to which one you prefer. Personally I find

Thumb Pick Worn on Thumb

- You need to figure out how much of the blade you want to expose to the string. If you wear the pick loosely you may get lots of noise when the thumb pick hits the string.

- Remember, don't wear the pick so tight that it hurts your thumb.

- Experiment with different size thumb picks with different sizes of blades.

Using Picks

- Hold the flat pick so that you are getting a good hit at the strings, but not so much that there is excessive pick noise.

- The flat pick is almost always held vertically, between the right thumb and the first finger.

- Some players also use the middle finger for support. This may make your wrist too tight for comfortable playing.

- You should expect that you will not feel as though you have much control over the pick until you have practiced using it for a while.

that metal thumb picks make too much noise for my taste.

Fingerpicks can be worn like rings on the index, middle, and ring fingers of the right hand, but some players skip the ring finger for reasons we'll go into later. Fingerpicks also come in both plastic and metal. The metal picks are made in different gauges of thickness. You can choose the one that feels and sounds the best to you.

Plastic Fingerpicks on Fingers

- When you put the picks on your fingers, don't expose too much of the pick.

- It is difficult to pick down while wearing picks, but it is not impossible to do so.

- If you use plastic fingerpicks, you will want to use a plastic thumb pick to match the sound.

Metal Fingerpicks on Fingers

- Metal fingerpicks can really make quite a bit of noise. You will have to spend some time controlling the sound.

- The main advantage of using metal fingerpicks is the ease of volume and speed that you get.

- The downside of metal fingerpicks is the inability to play softly without excessive string noises.

23

THE CAPO

The capo is a mechanical device that changes the key of a tune

Capos are used to change the key of a song by simply sliding the metal device up and down the fingerboard. Many different sorts of capos are currently available. They generally fall into two categories, elastic or fastened with a spring attachment. Each style of capo has its proponents. Generally what guitarists prefer is a capo that is easy to move quickly.

Jazz guitarists tend to make fun of capos, referring to them as "cheaters." What they are really saying is that players who use capos are too lazy to learn all of the possible chord positions on the fingerboard.

It is silly to automatically reject the use of capos. I once did a recording session that featured the country group the Statler Brothers. They were singing in C♯. I was playing banjo, and used a capo to transpose from the key of C to the key of C♯.

Elastic Capo—Used for Changing Keys

Spring Capo

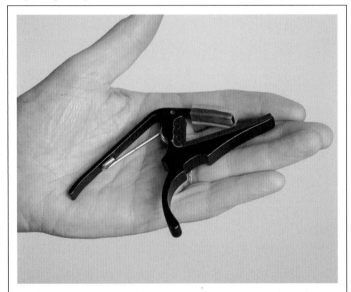

- The elastic capo is very easy to move, and is inexpensive.

- Elastic capos may not provide enough pressure on the strings to get a good sound.

- You never have to worry about elastic capos damaging the guitar neck.

- Elastic capos are a bit harder to find nowadays.

- The spring capo provides more pressure on the guitar neck.

- Some spring capos are quite moveable. Others require that you screw and unscrew the capo. For a performer, this is an inconvenience.

- There are a number of spring capos available. Select the one that you are comfortable using, and that provide sufficient pressure on the string to make a good sound.

The guitarist, an excellent jazz player, did not even own a capo, so he insisted on playing the song without one. In the left-hand fingerings he was using, it was impossible to play country-sounding chords with open strings. He proved that he could play without a capo, but he sounded awful.

Capos are particularly useful for singers, because they enable the singer to move a song up to a higher key without having to learn a new musical arrangement for the guitar.

Another reason for using the capo emerges when you start to play with other guitarists. If both guitarists are at an early level of skill development, one guitarist can play without a capo, and another guitarist can accompany him in another simple key, using a capo to play high on the neck of the guitar. The sound can be very attractive, like a small orchestra.

Elastic Capo on Guitar

- It is very simple to place the elastic capo on the guitar.

- Make sure that you have attached the elastic tightly enough so that it won't pop off the guitar.

- Always keep the capo just behind the fret that you are moving it to.

Spring Capo Placed on Guitar Neck

- Be careful not to scratch the guitar neck when you put the spring capo on.

- Make sure that the capo moves easily up and down the guitar neck.

- Check to make sure that it is easy to use the spring device.

SLIDES

Slide guitar is an exciting blues technique, used on many blues and rock recordings

Blues guitar playing developed sometime in the period between 1880 and 1900. The style of blues used in the Mississippi Delta is a very intense sort of instrumental and vocal music. Some of the early players like Son House used a pocketknife or a piece of a wine bottle held in the left hand to get a characteristic sound. Guitar accessory makers eventually began to sell glass, metal, and even ceramic slides to re-create this sound. Today slides are available in all of these configurations, as well as in various sizes. Some fit on the little finger of the left hand, and others are held in the entire left hand. Using a large slide that covers the whole hand makes for a very intense sound. However, slides that can be worn on

Metal Slide

- Metal slides, like other slides, come in different sizes. The size of the slide is important, because it determines how many strings the slide can play without the use of other left-hand fingers.

- Metal slides tend to get a very powerful sound. If you prefer a soft slide sound, they may not work for you.

- The smallest slides can only be used to play one or two strings, because the slide isn't wide enough to cover the width of the guitar neck.

Glass Slide

- Glass slides often are fashioned from old wine bottles.

- Glass slides have a somewhat gentler sound than their metal cousins.

- Glass slides are breakable, so be careful.

the little finger enable a guitarist to play other notes without a slide, in addition to the note that the slide is playing. Each technique has its advocates and practitioners.

The slide worn on the little finger can also produce another kind of sound. This is a somewhat sweet sound that is characteristic of Hawaiian guitar music. In this technique the guitarist plays a lot of single notes and uses vibrato in the left hand. Vibrato is a way of extending the length of the note by using the left hand in a sort of fluttery motion on a single fret. You can hear an example on the accompanying audio track.

Among contemporary guitarists, Ry Cooder is widely regarded as one of the best, or possibly the very best of slide players. He has written movie scores that incorporate this technique, notably his score for the film *Paris, Texas,* and he also has played slide guitar on a number of his own recordings, varying from his work with the Cuban Buena Vista Social Club to a number of recordings issued under his own name.

Ring Slide, Worn on Finger Like a Ring

- Ring slides are yet another variation.

- The sort of style that you prefer depends upon the sound that you are seeking. Try them all out!

Various Slides

- Some of the smaller slides are worn on the little finger. This enables the other fingers to play individual notes without the slides. A player can go from slide notes to chords that combine the use of the slide with the use of the left-hand fingers.

- Make sure that whatever slide you use fits properly. You don't want the slide to flop around while you are playing, and you don't want such a tight fit that it hurts your left-hand fingers.

GUITAR GEAR

SLIDES & PICK GUARDS

This section explores slide playing and discusses the function of the pick guard

There are two basic ways of wearing the slide on the left hand. In one technique, the slide covers the entire left-hand little finger. In the other method, enough of the finger is exposed that the player can alternate between playing with the slide and using the tip to finger the strings without the slide. The second technique is a bit of a tricky business, because it is difficult to avoid the feeling that the slide is getting in the way.

Players argue about which sort of slide produces a better sound. Some are sold on the glass slides, some of which are actually made from wine bottles. Others prefer the brass slides because they are much heavier and provide a more Delta

Slide Worn on Ring Finger of LH

- If you wear the slide on your left ring finger, you can use the first two fingers of the left hand to play other notes or even chords.

- You will not however be able to use the little finger of the left hand, because the slide will get in the way.

- Some players find the little finger of the left hand awkward to use, which is why they wear the slide on the ring finger.

Slide Worn on Little Finger of LH

- With the slide on the little finger, you have three fingers of the left hand free to play chords or other notes.

- If you tend to use the slide only on the higher strings,

you may want to consider buying a medium-size slide.

- Remember to finger all notes with the slide *exactly on the fret,* not behind the fret.

blues sort of a sound. The proponents of the slides that are worn on the pinky like the ability to use or not use the slide. Those guitarists are more apt to use the slide as an occasional device, rather than a tool for consistent blues playing.

If you purchase the sort of slide that you wear on the finger, you should be careful that the slide fits snugly, but not so tight as to make you feel as though you are cutting off the circulation to that finger.

The function of the pick guard is to protect the guitar against a player wearing through its top surface by playing hard. This can be the result of heavy-handed flat picking, or by playing too hard with fingerpicks.

Another function of the pick guard is as a place to rest the right elbow. Latin-American guitarists often use the top of the guitar as a sort of auxiliary percussion instrument. Once again the pick guard will protect the guitar against the consistent use of this technique.

Protective Pick Guard on Face of Guitar

- The pick guard protects the face of the guitar against wear from using a pick or a fingerpick.

- Make sure that the pick guard is attached tightly to the face of the guitar.

- If you never use any sort of picks, you may not want to bother with a pick guard.

Pick Guard Protecting Top of Guitar from Pick

- Pick guards are also used by players who tap on a guitar. This is a common technique in both flamenco and Latin-American music.

- Pick guards are inexpensive. Some are glued on the guitar, while some are attached with the use of materials similar to Velcro.

- If you do not use a pick guard, and play hard with some sort of pick, you can actually wear through the top of the guitar.

NECK SIZE & ACTION
The neck action and size are critical for comfortable playing

The width of the guitar's neck and the action (height of the string off the fingerboard) are essential matters to keep a guitar playing smoothly.

If you take your guitar to a competent repair person, the technician will immediately look at a number of issues that could be causing the action of the guitar to be too high (or too low).

First of all, the bridge may be too high, so that it needs to be replaced or sanded down. Sometimes it isn't the bridge that is the problem, but the nut at the other end of the guitar. It also may be too high or too low. If it is too high, it can be sanded down or replaced. The latter solution is likely if the nut is cut too low. Sometimes the nut is cut unevenly, so that some strings are higher than others, for no intelligent reason.

Neck Size Appropriate for Size of Player's LH

- The size of the neck needs to relate closely to the size of the player's left hand.

- There are so many models of guitar currently available, that any player should be able to find an appropriate size guitar. There are models of guitars for children that vary from ¼

normal size all the way up to the standard hand size of an adult. Remember that if you buy a tiny guitar for a small child, they will probably outgrow that instrument very quickly, and you will find yourself buying another instrument.

Neck Size Inappropriate for Size of Player's LH

- This guitar doesn't suit the size of the player's hand.

- Inappropriate guitar sizes lead to a player becoming discouraged. The guitar will not sound good, the player can have sore hands, and the guitar may even be difficult for the player to hold. Chances are that the

player will soon abandon the guitar.

- Inexperienced players who buy a guitar from a catalog or the Internet won't know how it will feel until they are actually holding it.

Once again, these problems are often found in mass-produced guitars. Some of the Asian guitar factories produce hundreds of guitars a day, too many to maintain effective quality control.

All of the problems described above are relatively easy and inexpensive to solve. A more serious situation occurs when the neck of the guitar is warped. A talented luthier can solve the problem of a guitar's neck being bowed. This however is an expensive and time-consuming process, and should be reserved for expensive vintage guitars that are worthy of being saved. In the case of an inexpensive guitar, this sort of treatment will cost more than the price of the guitar.

LH Playing on an Appropriate Size Neck

- Easy action has the opposite effect to what we described in the last section. The player will want to play more, because it is fun.

- Remember, if the action is too easy, the guitar will make annoying buzzing sounds.

- Your teacher is a good resource to determine whether the action is suitable for you.

LH Playing Guitar with Too High Action

- Difficult action is going to lead to a quick end to your career as a guitarist!

- Difficult action may be correctable by a competent repair person, but in the case of an inexpensive guitar, it may not be cost effective.

- Action can be affected by changes of temperature. Remember to keep your guitar away from heating vents or fireplaces.

CHANGING THE STRINGS
The sound of a guitar is strongly affected by the age of the strings

New guitars are usually equipped with new strings. If you purchase a new guitar, and the lining of the strings is worn, be sure to ask the store to put a new set of strings on the guitar. Your logical next question is: How do I know when to change the strings? If you see any sign of wear in the string, or if the guitar starts to sound dull to you, then it is probably time to change the strings. If your hands sweat regularly,

you may want to buy some string wipes to remove the sweat from the strings.

Changing steel strings is a relatively simple process. To remove a string that is on the guitar, simply tune the string down and then unwind it from the tuning post. Then remove the other end of the string by taking the pin out of the bridge. To install a new string follow the same process in an opposite

Steel String Being Changed, at the Bridge

- Be careful when handling steel strings. It is easy to cut your fingers on them.

- You need to hold the string in place while you are tuning it, or the end pin will come loose and the string will come out of it.

- Always be sure that you are inserting the correct string. If you tune a string too high, it will break.

Steel String Inserted into Hole

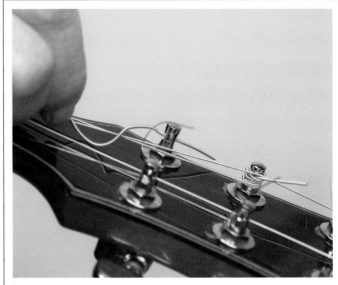

- You need to wind the string around the tuning peg, and then insert it into the hole.

- It's a good idea to cut some of the extra string length off with wire cutters before you start tuning the guitar.

- Don't cut too much of the extra string length off, or you won't have enough left for proper tuning.

way. Insert the ball end where the old string was lodged and then replace the end pin. Then pull the string firmly and wind the other end of the string around the tuning gear. Wind the string around the post, and then cut off the extra length of the string with wire cutters. While you tune the string, you must hold the end pin in place so that it doesn't pop as the pitch of the string goes higher. Nylon strings are tied to the bridge, using a single loop. They are inserted into the tuning gears in the same way that steel strings are placed there.

Nylon String Wound Tied to Bridge

- The nylon string has to be knotted at the end of the bridge.

- If your knot is too small, the guitar will come loose from the knot, and you will have to tie it again.

- After a while you will get used to the annoyance of having to knot the string every time you change it.

Nylon String, Wound around Tuning Gear

- Nylon strings are annoying to tune, because they stretch quite a bit until they have been played for a while.

- Because nylon strings stretch so much, the initial tuning is both annoying and time consuming.

- Try different brands of strings until you find the one that suits your taste.

CARE & TUNING

33

AMPLIFIERS

Amplifiers can be used with acoustic-electric guitars or solid-body electric guitars

Amplifiers are used to increase the volume of the guitar, or to modify the sound of the instrument.

Amplifiers range from tiny little battery-operated models that weigh less than ten pounds to monster-sized beasts with massive speakers used by superstar rock bands at arena concerts.

Some acoustic guitars simply have electronic pickups inserted in the sound holes. For the player who simply wants to use the amplifier to increase the volume of the instrument, they can simply plug the guitar into the amp and turn it on. More adventurous players may wish to adjust some of the knobs on the amplifier that increase treble, bass, or mid-

Small Guitar Amplifier

Medium-size Amplifier

- The guitar amplifier gives you increased volume, and if it is a quality amp, a variety of possible sounds.

- Small guitar amplifiers are great in terms of portability. There are even battery amps that weigh virtually nothing.

- Small amps don't have

unlimited volume or effects on them. If that's what you're looking for, you'll need to go with bigger, more expensive, and heavier models.

- You will need to buy a cord. One end plugs into your guitar, the other end goes into the amplifier. Cords come in varying lengths.

- Medium-size amplifiers have more effects and can be played louder than the smaller models.

- Your choice of amp depends upon the sounds that you enjoy, together with your guess about the sort of places where you may be playing. If you never play

outside your living room, you don't need a giant amp, unless your living room is the size of a small house!

- Be sure to try your own guitar with the amp you buy, to make sure the amp sounds good with your particular instrument.

range sounds, add echo or delay, etc.

Other acoustic-electric guitars have built-in electronics, and the player can adjust the sounds on the guitar itself, and further modify the sound by adjusting the amp.

Solid-body electric guitars may have multiple electronic pickups that produce fairly extreme sound possibilities that can be further modified with the amplifier or the many available foot pedals. These pedals create swooshing effects, wah-wah sounds, and all sorts of other sound effects.

To use an amplifier you must also purchase a cord that connects the guitar to the amplifier. Many types of cords are available, including ones that are quite long. They enable the player to move around the stage, or even to go into the audience. If you are using a guitar cord, it is always a good idea to make sure that it is functioning without any rattles or other glitches before you do a show.

Acoustic-electric Guitar Plugged into Amp

- Acoustic-electric guitars generally cannot be played with the sort of deafening volumes that rock stars use on solid-body electric guitars.

- You want an acoustic-electric guitar to produce a sound not unlike the acoustic instrument without the

amp. In other words, you're looking for a clean and pure sound. If you want a super-electronic sound, you should be playing a solid-body electric guitar.

- Some pickups go right into the sound hole of the guitar, some are attached through the end pin.

Amplifier with Electric Cord Visible

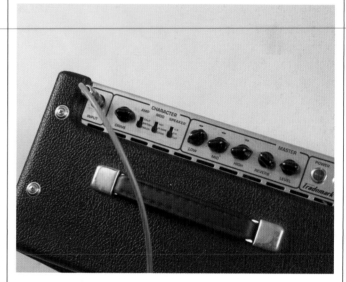

- Acoustic-electric guitars with built-in electronics are a good compromise for the player who usually wants to play acoustic guitar, but likes to rock out on occasion.

- The onboard electronics usually include choices

that allow increased or decreased treble, bass, and mid-range sounds.

- The electronics also often include echo or delay effects.

35

GUITAR CASES & GUITAR STANDS

Cases and stands are essential for maintaining and protecting your guitar

Guitar cases should be used whenever you have finished playing the guitar for the day, or when you take the guitar out of the house. Because so many guitars are in use, there are a large number of cases in different styles available.

There are four basic sorts of cases. Hardened professionals who do extensive touring use heavy fiberglass classes that

are virtually impregnable to any sort of mistreatment. These things are built like tanks, and are about as heavy as that sort of military hardware. They also cost hundreds of dollars.

The so-called hard-shell case is a solidly constructed case that is more than adequate for most challenges. Since these cases cost $100 to $150, if your guitar cost you $150, this is

Hard Case

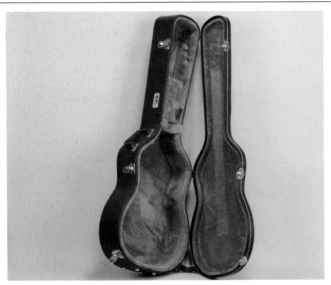

- Hard cases are substantially made wooden cases that protect guitars from most accidents.

- Be sure that the guitar fits comfortably in the case. It should not be too loose, or the guitar will bounce around, nor should it be too tight, or the guitar may

have no play at all if the case falls over.

- The guitar case is closed by metal clips. Some guitars have these clips on the back as well as the front. Make sure all of the clips are secured after you put the guitar in the case.

Gig Bag

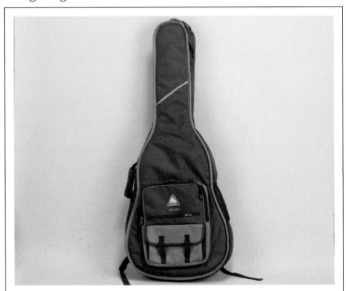

- A gig bag is a cloth bag that holds the guitar. It is very convenient, because it is usually quite light.

- Some professional players use gig bags that are quite heavy, although they are still lighter than hard

cases. It's not unusual to see bicycle riders wearing gig bag cases on their backs.

- Usually the airlines will allow you to carry on your gig bag.

probably more protection than you need or want. Chipboard cardboard cases are much cheaper, and certainly adequate for use around the house or in casual playing situations.

Gig bags are very popular among professional musicians. Some are heavy leather bags that hold guitars, and others are made of vinyl. In *most* instances you can carry a gig bag on an airplane. On the other hand I have also successfully carried hard cases on airplanes.

Guitar stands are useful if you like to leave your guitar out of the case, or if you perform with multiple instruments.

ZOOM

About the airlines: I once did a gig in Canada, and came home on the airlines to Denver with a well-known guitarist who got off to change planes there. I saw a baggage person *throw* this poor fellow's vintage guitar on an airline cart.

Cardboard Case

Guitar in Hard Case

- Cardboard cases are very light and are a reasonable alternative for moderate-priced instruments that aren't going to travel very much.

- The biggest advantage of cardboard cases is that they are relatively inexpensive.

- Cardboard cases don't offer much protection for your guitar. So don't pile your guitar in a car trunk and place heavy objects on top of it.

- Make sure the guitar fits properly in the case. It shouldn't be too tight or too loose.

- If any of the metal clips break, be sure to replace them.

- If the handle of your case is loose, be sure to replace it. I have had several experiences with handles breaking and the guitar case falling on the ground.

CARE & TUNING

ELECTRONIC TUNERS

Modern-day guitarists can use electronic tuners to assist them in tuning the guitar

This discussion will be restricted to tuning the guitar either to itself or with the aid of an electronic tuner. To tune the guitar in relationship to itself, you need to walk through the following steps. The metal bars that run horizontally up and down the fingerboard are called frets.

You will be tuning the guitar in relation to the lowest, 6th

string. Place a left-hand finger at the 6th string at the 5th fret. Tune the open 5th string to that note. (An open string is one that you play with the right hand without using any left-hand fingers.) Next place a left-hand finger at the 5th string at the 5th fret, and tune the open 4th string to that note. To tune the open 3rd string, you place a left-hand finger at the 4th string,

Small Electronic Tuner

- Electronic tuners are great, because they are accurate and very portable. The smaller ones are quite reasonably priced.

- When you use the electronic tuner, hit the guitar strings at a consistent level

- of volume. Otherwise the tuner becomes confused, and it may not give you accurate readings.

- Always carry extra batteries for your guitar tuner.

Larger Electronic Tuner

- Some of the larger tuners are more accurate, because the dials don't jump around as much after you hit a note.

- Larger tuners are more expensive than the small ones.

- Alternatives to using tuners are tuning to the piano or other instruments, or using a pitch pipe or a tuning fork. None of them are as convenient as electronic tuners.

5th fret. Now comes the only surprise. To tune the open 2nd string place a left-hand finger at the 3rd string at the *4th fret*. Finally, to tune the 1st string, place a left-hand finger at the 2nd string at the 5th fret. Note: Your guitar is now in tune to itself, but not to other instruments.

The tuner has electronic dials. When the dial is exactly in the middle, the note is in tune. If the dial veers to the left, the note is flat and should be tuned higher. If the note is sharp, the dial will veer to the right, and the string needs to be tuned lower.

ZOOM

Here is a useful tip for tuning. If you are in doubt whether to tune a string up or down, always tune it down. The reason for this is very simple. If you tune a string too high, it will break, and you will have to replace the string. Don't be intimidated by tuning. It takes some time before tuning becomes something of an automatic and tension-free task.

Tuner Mounted on Guitar

- Some smaller tuners can be mounted on the headstock of the guitar. This is a great convenience.

- When the tuner is mounted, extraneous outside noises will not interfere with the tuner. Other tuners don't work well when there are noises, such as those one would expect when playing outdoors.

- Many tuners have more than one available pitch. Make sure that you are using the 440 button on the tuner.

Tuner Dials Moving as Player Strikes String

- When the note is in tune, the pointer on the dial rests exactly in the middle of the tuner. If the pointer veers to the right the note is too high (sharp); if it is too low (flat), the pointer will veer to the left.

- Once again, don't hit the strings too hard, or the dial will flutter back and forth. Some tuners have other dials that you can use for other guitar tunings. Be sure that you are *not* using these dials unless you need them.

GUITAR PARTS

It is important to be able to identify the various parts of the guitar

Just as you need to know the difference between a car's engine and its brake system, it is a good idea to get to know the parts of a guitar. The sound of a guitar is influenced by the type of wood that has been used on the guitar's neck, sides, and back. Earlier we mentioned that many players are partial to the sound of rosewood guitars. These days the rosewood is usually imported from India or Africa. Spruce tops are common, and another wood used is mahogany. Mass-produced guitars often use some wood and laminated materials between the layers of wood.

Laminated materials do not change over time, but one of the reasons that old rosewood guitars are in favor is that over time they produce a mellow and attractive sound that is difficult to duplicate in a new guitar. Mass-produced guitars

Guitar Parts

- Here are the various parts of the guitar: The bridge holds the strings on the guitar, with the strings attached over the saddle.

- The rosette of the guitar is the fancy engraving around the sound hole.

- By this time, you are most likely familiar with most of the parts of the guitar.

Back of Guitar

- The back of the guitar is what rests against you when you play the instrument with your right hand.

- The back can be made of rosewood, mahogany, or other woods.

- Less expensive guitars have laminates, several sections of wood glued together.

- The cheapest guitars use plywood.

almost invariably use the lamination process, which is obviously cheaper for the manufacturer.

The headstock of the guitar is the place where the tuning gears live. If the tuning gears are loose, they will not hold the guitar strings in tune. Sometimes a simple turn of the screw with a small screwdriver will correct this problem.

The height of the saddle over the guitar bridge will be one of the main determinants of the ease of guitar action. From time to time make sure that the bridge of the guitar is not loose, or coming up from the guitar body. If you notice that this is happening, be sure to take the guitar to a competent repair person to glue it back. If the bridge is not placed properly on the guitar, the relationship between the strings will be affected, and the guitar will not play in tune.

Headstock of Guitar

- The headstock of an expensive guitar is often inlaid.

- The tuners rest on the headstock.

- Many manufacturers use identifying corporate logos on the headstock.

Bridge of Guitar

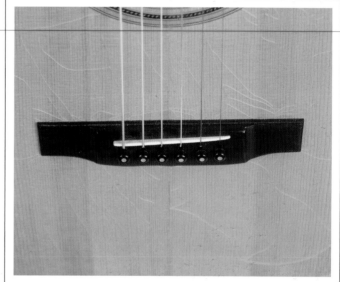

- Bridges are glued onto the body of the guitar.

- The strings rest over the saddle, on top of the bridge.

- Underneath the bridge is a bridge plate, glued under the bridge to provide support.

GUITAR STRAPS

A strap is an essential tool for anyone who plays the guitar while standing

If you play the guitar while standing, it is essential that you purchase a guitar strap. Straps come in many sizes, materials, and colors. Leather straps are quite sturdy, but also tend to be fairly heavy. Cloth straps are lighter, and often come in a variety of colors and designs. Any music store that has a decent stock of guitars should have a good supply of guitar straps.

It is important that you adjust the strap so that the guitar is secured at a height that enables you to move your arms without difficulty. If the strap is high up on your chest, it will be awkward to move your wrists. Your wrist may actually become sore from playing the guitar positioned too close to your body. On the other hand, if the guitar is worn too low,

Leather Straps

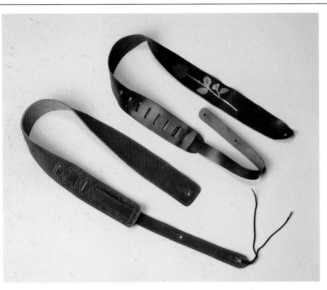

- Leather straps are quite sturdy, and offer good support for the guitar.

- Leather is always rather heavy, and you may prefer a lighter material.

- Many ornate designs are now available.

Cloth Straps

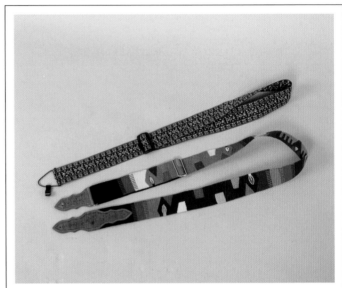

- Cloth straps are much lighter than leather ones.

- By the same token, cloth straps offer less support for the guitar.

- Many colorful cloth patterns are now available.

you will have little control over your playing. It will feel more like aimless flailing than concentrated effort. If you have ever seen any movies starring Elvis Presley, you may recall that he played his guitar so low on his body that it is hard to imagine how he was able play it at all.

Straps can also be used to support the guitar when you are seated. Some players enjoy the feeling that their guitars are secure and do not have to be supported by their bodies.

The strap is attached to the end pin of the guitar, the little pin at the tip of the guitar beyond the bridge. Most guitars come with an end pin. If you don't have one, and you wish to use a strap, you will need to get a repair person to drill a hole that will enable the end pin to be inserted. The other end of the strap is attached above the nut of the guitar.

Strap Attached to Back of Guitar

- It is essential that the strap is securely attached, or it may come loose.

- If the guitar comes loose it will fall, and unless the player happens to catch it, it may be seriously damaged.

- It is important that the player adjust the strap so that it leaves the guitar at an appropriate place on the body while standing.

- If the guitar is set either too high or too low, it will be uncomfortable to play.

Other End of Guitar Strap Attached to End Pin

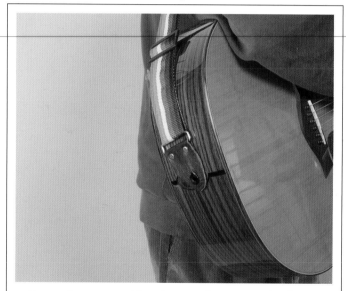

- Most guitars come with end pins that will hold the strap.

- Always make sure that the end pin itself is securely attached, and that the guitar strap is also firmly in place.

- End pins can be purchased at any music store.

43

STANDING & SITTING

Although many performers stand while playing, it is easier to play the guitar when you are seated

If you wish to play the guitar standing up, but you don't like to wear a strap, you will probably have to bend your knee and place it on a chair or some other slightly elevated surface. Balancing the guitar in this playing position is awkward, but eventually you will get the hang of supporting it against your chest.

If you use a guitar strap while standing, make sure that the strap is tightly secured at both ends. Every guitar player has stories of guitars coming loose from straps while the player was in the middle of a hot solo. If a guitarist fails to notice that a strap is coming loose, the guitar may actually have a crash landing on the floor.

Player Standing Up without Strap

- If the player is standing up without a strap, it is necessary to support the guitar in some way. If the guitarist's leg is on a stool or bench, the guitar can be supported by the player's body.

- Playing standing up without a strap can be an invitation to dropping the guitar.

- The guitarist is probably better off sitting down than trying to play standing up without a strap.

Player Standing Up with Strap

- The key question is how high to "wear" the guitar on your body.

- If the guitar is not comfortable to play, then you need to readjust the strap up or down.

- You never want to wear the guitar too close to your body, or too far down.

If you are seated and playing without a strap, you can easily secure the instrument by holding it against your chest and also leaning against the instrument with your right elbow.

Classical guitarists like to raise the left leg higher than the right leg. They often perform with little foot stools, placing the left leg on the foot stool, but leaving the right foot on the ground.

If you are playing while seated, do not cross your legs. If you are playing for any length of time, this can actually cut off the circulation to your legs.

I have also seen a few guitarists who use a saxophone strap while playing. One end is attached against the sound hole of the guitar, the other end around the player's neck. I don't recommend this approach, particularly if the instrument is fairly heavy.

Player Holding Guitar, Seated with No Strap

- When the player is seated, it is possible to play without a strap. The guitar will be supported by the right elbow, and held against the chest.

- There is still some danger that the guitar may fall out of the player's hand.

- Remember, when seated, do not cross your legs.

Playing Holding Guitar, Seated with Strap

- If the player is seated with a strap, he or she must still determine exactly how high the guitar should be held above the body.

- If the strap is interfering with the freedom of your arm motions, do not use it.

- If you are seated with the strap on the guitar and then get up, you need to be careful that the guitar is secure.

45

LEFT-HAND POSITION
Beginners often find that positioning the left thumb is awkward

The left thumb always feels awkward to the beginning player. It isn't used for playing chords, so what should a guitarist do with it? In classical guitar technique, the thumb is positioned behind the fingerboard. This feels awkward at first, but after a while classical players get used to it. Many jazz and folk players position the thumb parallel to the fingerboard and those who have thumbs that are flexible may even use the left thumb for fingering chords. Classical guitarists tend to place the left hand in an arched position. The fingers are kept almost vertical, above the fingerboard. Jazz and folk guitar players tend to keep the left wrist much looser.

The most important aspect of left-hand fingering is that the wrist should not be too tense. A tense wrist will discourage you from practicing, and it can even lead to tendonitis. If

LH, Classical Position Thumb behind Neck

- The position of the left thumb should be relaxed, or your entire hand will become sore.

- For most players the thumb should be held not on the guitar neck, but just behind it.

- Remember to cut your left thumbnail.

LH, Classical Position, Other Fingers of LH

- In classical technique, the left thumb should never protrude over the neck.

- Do not use the left thumb to support the guitar.

- If the left thumb is tense, it will have a bad effect on your playing.

you find that your left wrist is tense, you are probably using a hand position that is not working well for you. Assuming that your guitar is in playable condition, if you have trouble changing chords, then there is a good chance that your left hand and wrist are causing the problem.

LH, Folk Position, Left Thumb over Neck

- Some country and folk players drape the left thumb over the strings.

- It is even possible to play bass notes with the left thumb.

- Once again, do not squeeze the left thumb against the neck for support.

Rest of LH in Folk Position

- It is possible to keep the left thumb relaxed, playing neither in classical position nor with the thumb right on the neck.

- The essential issue is, is your thumb position making your left hand tired?

- Try the different thumb positions.

- What works best for you?

RIGHT-HAND POSITION

The right-hand position has a profound effect on the tone that guitarists achieve

The position of the right hand in classical guitar playing differs from other ways of playing the instrument. In classical guitar the right hand is held in an arched position above the strings. The guitar is almost always picked up, or toward the player. The emphasis is on getting a clear sound, with each string sounding individually.

Sometimes the strings are plucked up toward the player, and another technique has each finger coming to rest on the next string. This technique absolutely requires the players to have functioning fingernails on the right hand.

There are a variety of hand positions used in folk, country, jazz, or blues playing, and of course many of these styles can

KNACK GUITAR FOR EVERYONE

RH Shown Arched, Classical Position

- In arched position, the right hand is held above the strings.

- With the right hand arched, you should be able to play very clear single notes.

- Arched position enables you to use the ring finger and even the little finger to play the strings.

Wrist Arched, Playing Strings

- Notice how high the right hand is above the strings.

- The combination of an arched wrist and smooth fingernails should enable

- you to achieve a good sound on the guitar.

- Don't arch your hand so much as to feel any sense of strain.

also be played with a flat pick, rather than by using the right-hand fingers. One hand position used in nonclassical playing is to curl the wrist. A different approach comes from resting the ring finger or little finger of the right hand against the pick guard. Of course, if you are resting the ring finger on the pick guard, you cannot use that finger for playing. On the other hand, if you do not want to use this finger anyway, that playing position is perfectly adequate.

Blues players often use only the thumb and one finger, or thumb and two fingers of the right hand.

Ultimately your right-hand position should reflect the sort of music or specific sound that you are striving to achieve, while also feeling comfortable.

RH, Nonclassical About to Play

- Nonclassical players tend to play with a less arched wrist position.

- You should still be able to achieve a good sound with this hand position.

- Don't rest any right-hand fingers on the guitar.

RH, Nonclassical Playing

- Notice how relaxed the hand is.

- Developing independence between the thumb and your right-hand fingers is important.

- You shouldn't have to make violent right-hand motions in your playing, unless you are striving for particular effects, as in flamenco guitar.

RIGHT-HAND PICK POSITION

Playing with a flat pick is a wholly different right-hand guitar technique

Flat picks are held in the right hand, usually between the thumb and first fingers of the guitar. There are picks of different sizes, different degrees of thickness, and different materials.

Flat picks enable the guitarist to play single note passages with great speed, or to strum very loudly on the guitar without damaging the fingernails of the right hand. Many jazz guitarists play exclusively with a pick, although others use a pick and fingers simultaneously.

When players begin to use a pick, the impulse is that it is going to fall out of the player's hand. Often this is exactly what happens. Over time you should develop a sense of greater security about holding the pick.

Flat Pick in RH, at Rest

- Hold the flat pick between the right thumb and index finger.

- Don't hold the hand too tight, or your wrist will become tense.

- Does the pick feel comfortable in your hand?

Flat Pick in RH, in Action

- You need to bend your right hand to pick the strings with the pick.

- You can come to rest on the next string, or lift the pick up, depending on what string the next note will be on.

- It is possible to play very rapidly with a flat pick without much effort.

A number of issues come up in pick-style playing. One of the biggest is how much of the pick should be exposed by the hand. In most styles of guitar playing, it is desirable to limit the amount of pick noise, so that players try to expose as little of the pick as possible.

Picks, like guitar strings, come in various gauges of thickness, and players have their individual preferences for extra light, light, medium or heavy gauge picks.

Another issue with picks is the shape of the pick. A few players actually like large, triangular picks, and there are also picks that have some sort of gripping material on the back that seeks to prevent a player from dropping the pick.

Angle of Pick Seen from Top

- This is a view from above the hand.

- Notice how bent the wrist is.

- Good flat pickers don't need a great deal of motion in their playing.

Angle from Pick Seen from Rear

- The view from behind shows the wrist bent from a different angle.

- Notice how the right-hand fingers are curled.

- The wrist moves slightly as the string is picked.

GUITAR STANDS & CLEANING CLOTHS
These are simple but valuable tools to protect your guitar

Guitar stands serve several purposes. Guitarists who perform on stage often play several different guitars, or play guitar and another instrument, like banjo, mandolin, or electric bass. A guitar stand enables the guitarist to place an instrument in the stand, so that it does not fall or become damaged. It is important that you carefully place the guitar in the stand, because if you do not do so, the guitar may fall out. The stand

should also be positioned so that the performer or other band members do not kick the guitar. In other words, the proper use of a guitar stand involves taking some common-sense precautions.

For the nonprofessional guitarist, the stand can be used in between practice sessions, or, for example, if you are in the middle of playing when the phone or the doorbell rings. It

Guitar Stand

- The guitar stand holds the guitar when you are not playing it.

- Guitar stands are useful on or off stage.

- A guitar can be left in the guitar stand in between playing sessions.

Guitar in the Stand

- If the guitar is not securely in place, the guitar can fall.

- Guitar stands come in different sizes and weights.

- Even if you have a guitar stand, put the guitar in its case at night.

is amazing how easy it is to leave the guitar leaning against a table or chair, only to have it fall down. If you have small children, guitar stands are also a practical way of protecting the guitar against a child banging into it.

Cleaning cloths provide a more subtle protection for your instrument. Anyone who notices that their hands sweat while playing the guitar can prolong the life of the strings by running the cloth over the frets. If you never clean the frets of the guitar, gunk may build up there, and actually impede your playing. Cloths are available at music stores.

When purchasing a guitar stand, it is a good idea to bring your guitar to the music store and place it in the stand, in order to make sure that the stand is a good fit for your particular instrument.

Guitar Cleaning Cloth

- Cleaning cloths protect the finish of the guitar.

- Cloths extend the life of strings by removing sweat.

- Cleaning cloths are inexpensive and widely available.

Guitar Cleaning Cloth in Use

- After you have finished playing, go over the frets of the guitar with the cloth.

- Cleaning cloths are essential tools if your hands sweat to any degree.

- Cleaning cloths also keep gunk from accumulating on the guitar neck.

D CHORD
In this section you will learn your first guitar chord

Playing the guitar requires you to learn how to coordinate your left and right hands. I am going to assume that whether you are left- or right-handed, you will be playing the strings with the right hand, and fingering the chord positions with your left hand. If you are a certified guitar genius, like Jimi Hendrix or folk guitarist Elizabeth Cotton, then you can play the guitar left-handed and upside down. Failing that degree

of talent and ingenuity, I strongly recommend that you follow the "normal" practice described above.

The first chord that you will learn is the D chord. This involves placing the index finger of your left hand at the 3rd string on the 2nd fret, your ring finger on the 2nd string at the 3rd fret, and your middle finger on the 1st string at the 2nd fret.

The sixth string is the one closest to your body, and lowest

D Chord from Behind

- It is vital that you arch the fingers of your left hand.

- Note that each finger of the left hand that is used here plays one string.

- If the sound is muffled, you are probably either not pressing hard enough, or your fingers are hitting more strings than the ones that they should be hitting.

D Chord

- Are you pressing hard enough with the left-hand fingers?

- Is your left thumb relaxed?

- Is your left hand getting tired?

in musical pitch of the six strings. For guitarists, the left hand has four fingers, the first is the index, the second is the middle, the third is the ring finger, and the fourth finger is the little finger.

In this book we will be presenting chords both through photos and diagrams. A diagram of the D chord is shown at the right.

ALWAYS place your left-hand fingers just *behind* the fret. Do not play the 6th string with this chord.

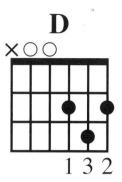

D

D Chord, Showing Left Wrist

- How does your left wrist feel?

- How does the left thumb feel?

- Is your left wrist arched?

D Chord, Showing Position of Left Thumb

- Where is your left thumb?

- What happens when you move the left thumb?

- How does your wrist feel when you move the left thumb?

A7 CHORD
You will now learn the A7 chord

The A7 chord only involves the use of two fingers of the left hand. The middle finger plays the 4th string at the 2nd fret, while the ring finger plays the 2nd string at the 2nd fret. You can play all six strings of the guitar using this chord. The chord diagram is below.

Your goal is to be able to go from one chord to the other without needing to look at the guitar.

This will not occur overnight. It takes quite a bit of practice. In the meantime, work at playing in a consistent rhythm. Start at a *slow* pace. For your right hand, brush down across the strings with your thumb, or with a flat pick. Do your best to play at a slow enough tempo that you don't have any pause between moving from one chord to the next.

Aim to clearly hear all of the strings of the guitar, including

Diagram of A7

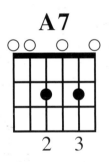

A7 Chord

- You can play the 6th string with this chord.

- Memorize this chord, so that you can move in and out of the chord without difficulty.

- This chord is easier to play than the D, because you only need to use two fingers of the left hand.

- Can you hear all of the strings clearly when you strum?

- Are you hearing any muffled strings?

- Does the chord sound good to you?

56

the open string that is not being fingered by the left hand, as well as the strings that you are fingering with the left hand. The most common difficulties occur with the D chord, because the A7 chord involves using only two fingers, and they are not playing on adjacent strings. If you get a fuzzy sound when fingering the D chord, the following things may be happening:

The fingers of your left hand are not arched high enough
You are not exerting enough pressure with the left hand. You shouldn't be pressing so hard that your left-hand fingers hurt.

A7 Chord, Showing Position of Left Wrist

- How does your wrist feel?
- Does each string sound clear?
- Are you fingering the correct strings?

A7 Chord, Showing Position of Left Thumb

- Where is your left thumb placed?
- Is your wrist loose or tight?
- What happens when you move your thumb?
- Are you comfortable playing the chord?

CHANGING CHORDS—D TO A7

Once you have mastered the D-A7 sequence, you will be ready for your first song

You are now at a critical time in your burgeoning career as a guitar player. If you can master the ability to go from one chord change to another without stopping or stuttering, you are well on your way to being able to play songs. The next portion of this book is designed to help you through the process of changing chords in rhythm.

Even though I haven't asked much of you in terms of what the right hand is supposed to do, I want to urge you to pay attention to playing a consistent rhythmic pattern with the right hand. The easiest way to do this is to count four beats, 1, 2, 3, 4. It may help you to tap your feet while you are doing this. Your goal is to play each chord four times without

D-A7

- Are you pausing when you change the chord?

- How does the D chord sound?

- Are you playing in rhythm?

- Is it getting easier to remember the chord?

D-A7

- The A7 chord should be easy for you to play by this time.

- How did it feel to change the chord?

- No strings should sound muffled.

missing a beat when you change from one chord to the next. Remember, you should be playing with the right thumb, or with a pick, playing down across the strings from the lower-pitched strings to the higher-pitched ones. Try this:

D///	D///	D///	D///
D///	D///	D///	D///
A7///	A7///	A7///	A7///
D///	D///	D///	D///

The slash line (/) indicates a strum.

D-A7

- Going back to the D chord is probably still a challenge.

- Keep your wrist relaxed,

- Don't get discouraged if the notes aren't really clear.

D-A7

- The A7 chord should be a relief.

- Are you keeping time, or do you pause when you change the chords?

- Your left hand may be getting tired now.

PRACTICING A7-D

The material in this sequence is intended to improve your ability to change chords

This section doesn't contain any new material. It is designed to reinforce your ability to change chords quickly and efficiently. Let's begin by reversing the pattern. This time, instead of changing from D to A7, go from A7 to D.

The sequence will look like this:

| A7/// | A7/// | A7/// | D/// |
| A7/// | A7/// | A7/// | D/// |

For your next practice session, try to play three beats for each chord, as though you were playing in waltz time. Play:

A7-D

- Not looking at the guitar is a challenge.

- If it's too confusing, look at the guitar every other time you play the chord.

- Don't play too fast.

A7-D

- If you can play the D chord without looking at it, you're well on the way.

- Don't speed up when you play.

- Try to keep your wrist relaxed.

D//   D//   D//   D//

A7//   A7//   A7//   D//

At this point, try to play the chords without looking at the chord. Look at the guitar only when you play the D chord, and try the rest of any of these sequences without looking at the neck of the guitar.

A7-D

- You're back at A7, that should come easy.

- Make sure you're fingering the correct notes of the chord.

- Try playing the sequence *slow*.

A7-D

- It is best to move the fingers of the left hand together, rather than one at a time. If you try to move them one at a time, the chances are you will not be playing in rhythm.

- Congratulate yourself for a good practice session.

- Before you know it, you'll be playing songs.

CHORD CHANGING PROBLEMS

These are some of the typical problems players experience in making chord changes

Remember that I promised that once you have mastered the ability to change chords I would introduce the first song. We're almost there! But first let's troubleshoot some of the typical problems that beginning guitarists are apt to experience at this stage of the game. The next four photos will illustrate four of these possible trouble spots, as follows:

The left hand is not arched high enough. This makes the strings overlap so that you are touching additional strings besides the ones that you are fingering in the left hand. This results in the notes being muffled, rather than clear.

The left wrist has the correct arch, but the left-hand fingers are still overlapping and hitting additional strings. Sometimes

Poor Wrist Arch in LH

- If the left hand arch collapses, your chords will sound muddy.

- Don't let the wrist get tense.

- Don't overarch the hand, or it may get tired.

LH Fingers Overlapping Strings

- When you overlap strings, the notes become muddy.

- Clarity is a must for a good sound.

- You should be able to start correcting yourself now.

this is a simple problem; the guitarist has neglected to cut the left-hand fingernails, and that is what is making the fingerings inaccurate.

The left thumb may interfere with your ability to stretch the left-hand fingers. You are not applying enough pressure with the left hand, either because you are not pressing hard enough, or because the guitar has been poorly set up, and it is difficult to press down on the chords. The guitar neck is either too wide or too narrow for your left hand. The strings are too heavy a gauge for you to finger them comfortably.

LH Fingering Chord Incorrectly

- Are you playing the correct notes?

- If the notes sound really muddy, you are probably fingering the wrong strings.

- The problem may be with your left thumb.

Another Poor LH Position

- How does the thumb feel?

- Is the thumb making your wrist tense?

- You should begin to feel that you have found the right position for your thumb.

WARPED NECKS & TRUSS RODS

If a guitar's neck is warped, it is very difficult to finger in the left hand

Sometimes over time guitar necks warp, and the height of the strings over the fingerboard makes it virtually impossible for the left-hand fingers to play the guitar.

Guitars can warp because they are kept too close to a heat source, or the player leaves the instrument out in the bright sunlight. Modern guitar makers use a truss rod, usually made of steel to prevent warping. The rod is inserted by the maker, and it runs the entire length of the guitar's neck.

The truss rod can be adjusted with a wrench to straighten the guitar neck when heat or simply the aging of the wood has created such problems. Gibson Guitars started to use steel truss rods in the early 1920s.

Warped Guitar Neck

- A warped neck is a serious problem.

- When you sight down the neck, it should be relatively straight.

- One sign of a warped neck is that when you play up the neck of the guitar, the notes sound out of tune.

Guitar Truss Rod Used to Straighten Neck

- The truss rod is barely visible at the neck near the tuning keys.

- The truss rod is a rod that runs the length of the neck of your guitar.

- Not all guitars have truss rods.

- There is more than one truss rod design.

When a truss rod is loosened, the strings are pulled forward. Tightening the rod has the opposite effect.

If you sight down the neck and it is clearly warped, it is a good idea to bring the guitar to a qualified repair person. If you own a vintage guitar that has a badly warped neck, it is possible to straighten the neck out by heating the guitar, but this is an expensive and time-consuming process that not all guitar repair people have mastered. Even if you are a do-it-yourself kind of person, I strongly recommend that you talk to a qualified repair person.

Another View of Guitar Truss Rod

- The truss rod can help your guitar stay free from major repairs.

- The guitar's action can also be adjusted without a truss rod, by lowering or raising the saddle, or re-carving the nut.

Wrench Used to Adjust Truss Rod

- The wrench turns the truss rod.

- Using the wrench without knowing what you are doing is a serious error. You can really hurt the guitar neck.

- It's best to let a repair person do any neck adjustments.

RIGHT THUMB OR PICK
It's time to introduce some right-hand playing techniques

In this chapter you will begin to learn how to use the right hand. To start with, we will simply go over what we have already covered.

Extend the right thumb out horizontally from the rest of your right hand. Remember that when you play the D chord, do not play the 6th (lowest-pitched) string of the guitar. Brush across the strings in a sort of windmill pattern. Remember to keep the tempo even, and to pat your foot on each beat.

After you brush across the strings, lift the thumb back without playing, and prepare for the next strum.

If you become bored with the strum, alternate between using the thumb to brush down across the string, and then back. Keep the rhythm even.

Next we are going to do exactly the same strum pattern,

Right Thumb Preparing to Brush Down

- Hold the right thumb up over the string.

- Strum evenly, not too fast.

- How does it sound?

Right Thumb Brushing Down across Strings

- The right thumb moves down across the strings.

- Remember, don't play the lowest (6th) string when you are fingering a D chord.

- Don't hit the pick guard of the guitar with your thumb.

- Keep the thumb relaxed.

but instead of using the right thumb, playing with a flat pick placed between your right thumb and index finger. Notice that by using the pick you can play loud and strong without much effort.

Try to avoid getting too much pick noise. To do this, don't expose too much of the pick. The more the body of the pick brushes across the strings, the more pick noise you will hear.

As with the thumb brush, when you become bored using the pick to play down, alternate between down and up picking. You will quickly notice that it is a bit more difficult

to strum upwards (toward you) with the pick. If you practice alternating picks for a while, the problem will go away.

Pick About to Brush Down

- Hold the pick securely, but not too tight.

- Don't bang on the guitar with the pick.

- Play steadily.

Pick Brushing Down

- Play in rhythm, four beats at a time.

- Don't slow down or speed up.

- Do the notes sound clear to you?

- If the notes don't sound good, check your left hand.

DOWN & UP STRUMMING

In this section you will begin to refine alternating down and up strumming

In the previous section, I suggested that if you became bored with down picking, that you could begin to alternate picking down and up. That is exactly what you will be doing here.

Start by using the right thumb. You have executed the down pick with the thumb extended horizontally from the rest of the hand. Follow this down pick by brushing back with the thumb across the strings from the highest-pitched string to the lower ones. If you are feeling comfortable about changing chords, speed up the chord changes. Try playing two beats of D followed by two beats of A7. Mix things up to amuse yourself. Play two beats of D, followed by four beats of A7.

Thumb Brushes Down

- Set up a 4/4 rhythm, count 1, 2 , 3, 4.

- Keep time and don't rush.

- Play evenly.

- Brush down across most of the strings.

Thumb Brushes Back

- Brushing back is more difficult.

- It's fine if you don't hit all of the bass strings.

- Curl your thumb on the way back up.

- Keep time!

Occasionally try three beats. The Beatles were particularly ingenious about mixing up rhythms. Changing rhythms during a song provides an interesting way of surprising the listener's ear. It adds spice to the listener's experience.

Next once again pick up the flat pick. Just as you did with the right thumb, alternate up and down picking. Play evenly, and try to hit as many strings with your up picks as you did with the down picks. This is a bit harder to do than it sounds, because the up-picking motion is a bit awkward.

Just as when you were using the thumb strum, mix the rhythms up. Play two beats of D, followed by four beats of A7. If you're finding all of this to be pretty elementary, then really mix the rhythms up. Play the D chord with a long note (quarter note) picking down, then pick two short (eighth) notes, starting with the up pick, followed quickly by a down pick. The rhythm is: 1 2&, 1 2&, etc.

Pick Brushes Down

- This is the same operation that you just performed with your thumb, but now you're using a pick.

- Does the pick feel secure in your hand?

- Your right wrist should be relaxed.

Pick Brushes Back

- Brushing back with the pick is more difficult.

- It's fine if you only play three or four strings on the way back.

- Keep time.

- Experiment by playing loud, then soft.

CHORD CHANGES & STRUMS

By the end of the next two sections, you will have integrated simple strums with chord changes

We're going to integrate a variety of rhythms with the things you have learned about chord changes and strums. I'm also going to place the chord changes in different places, so that you get lots of practice on how you go about making the changes while strumming, without slowing down.

The goals of the next three sections of the book are to enable you to play in different rhythms without struggling, to integrate strums with chord changes, and to move back and forth between using your fingers (in this case finger) and a flat pick.

My experience has been that the sooner a guitarist learns how to play with both the pick and the fingers of the right

If you can master changing chords in rhythm, you're on your way.

Be sure your left-hand fingerings are correct.

Don't play the 6th string with D.

Try not to look at the guitar.

4/4

D///	D///	D///	D///
D///	D///	D///	D///
D///	D///	D///	D///
D///	D///	D///	D///

Did you change the chord in tempo?

Did you have to look at the chord?

Are you keeping good time?

Are you ready to change again?

4/4

A7///	A7///	A7///	A7///
A7///	A7///	A7///	A7///
A7///	A7///	A7///	A7///
A7///	A7///	A7///	A7///

Were you able to get back to D in time?

Are the notes clear?

Is your left hand getting tired?

hand, the easier it will be for him or her to switch back and forth between these right-hand techniques.

Most players are clearly better at either playing with the pick or with the fingers. Eventually you too will probably find one technique more comfortable, or simply prefer the way that it sounds.

My goal is to help you develop to the point where you are roughly equally capable of both styles, and you can make your choice based on your musical taste, rather than the limitations of your right-hand technical abilities.

Note: 4/4 time means there are four beats for each measure of music.

Are you ready to change to 2/4, two beats to the measure?

2/4

D/   D/   A.7/   A.7/

D/   D/   A.7/   D/

D/   D/   A.7/   A.7/

D/   D/   A.7/   D/

D/   D/   A.7/   A.7/

D/   D/   A.7/   D/

D/   D/   A.7/   A.7/

D/   D/   A.7/   D

If you got even close to making the chord changes in time, you're doing great.

The second line is particularly tough.

Try this with your thumb and also with a pick.

Get ready to go back to 4/4.

4/4

A.7///   A.7///   D

A.7///   A.7///   D

A.7///   A.7///   D

The second line has frequent chord changes.

Try not to look at the guitar.

Critique your own playing. Does it sound good to you?

A.7///   D///   A.7///   D///

A.7///   D///   A.7///   D///

A.7///   D///   A.7///   D///

A.7///   D///   A.7///   D///

MIXING IT UP
We will mix up the rhythms a bit more here

The chord changes are going to fly by in this section. Don't be surprised to find yourself playing a chord for a single beat. Your initial reaction will probably be that you can't possibly do it. There's nothing here that you haven't already tried, it's just that the chord changes come more and more rapidly. To steal a line from President Obama, "Yes you can!"

All that it takes is a bit of concentration, together with the degree of right- and left-hand coordination that you have been working on throughout this book.

Remember to tap your foot in a regular rhythm. If at all possible, record your playing on your computer, some sort of digital recording device, or even a cassette recorder. When you play back the recording, try to determine whether you are keeping time.

4/4			
D///	D///	D/A7/	D///
D///	A7///	DA7D/	A7///
DA7DA7	A7///	D/A7D	D///
DA7DA7	A7///	A7DA7D	D///

D///	D///	D/A7/	D///
D///	A7///	DA7D	A7///
DA7DA7	A7///	D/A7D	D///
DA7DA7	A7///	A7DA7D	D///

D///	D///	D/A7/	D///
D///	A7///	DA7D/	A7///
DA7DA7	A7///	D/A7D	D///
DA7DA7	A7///	A7DA7D	D///

D///	D///	D/A7/	D///
D///	A7///	DA7D/	A7///
DA7DA7	A7///	D/A7D	D///
DA7DA7	A7///	A7DA7D	D///

If you know anyone who plays piano, guitar, or drums, try to get them to play along with you. The point of recording your playing is that it is much easier to evaluate your playing when you can simply listen and not have to play at the same time.

Playing with other musicians will greatly improve your ability to keep time.

4/4

DA7/D	A7DA7D	D////	A7////
A7D/A7	D////	D/A7/	D//A7
A7DA7D	D/A7D	D////	A7////
DA7/D	D/A7D	A7//D	D////

DA7/D	A7DA7D	D////	A7////
A7D/A7	D////	D/A7/	D//A7
A7DA7D	D/A7D	D////	A7////
DA7/D	D/A7D	A7//D	D////

DA7/D	A7DA7D	D////	A7////
A7D/A7	D////	D/A7/	D//A7
A7DA7D	D/A7D	D////	A7////
DA7/D	D/A7D	A7//D	D////

DA7/D	A7DA7D	D////	A7////
A7D/A7	D////	D/A7/	D//A7
A7DA7D	D/A7D	D////	A7////
DA7/D	D/A7D	A7//D	D////

DA7/D	A7DA7D	D////	A7////
A7D/A7	D////	D/A7/	D//A7
A7DA7D	D/A7D	D////	A7////
DA7/D	D/A7D	A7//D	D////

MORE MIXING

The more you get used to playing in different patterns, the easier it becomes to do it

Next you will have a chance to make your chord changes in different meters, as well as making the chord changes on different beats of the musical measure. Remember that 4/4 time means that there are four beats to a measure of music, 2/4 indicates that there are two beats to the measure, and 3/4, or waltz time, has three beats to each measure of music.

By mixing up these rhythms you will begin to understand that learning how to play is only an exercise in adding various musical layers. Imagine it as a cooking exercise, where we are continually adding ingredients to make the taste more pleasing. That's exactly the way that your playing should be developing. We began with some instruction in playing

---

Watch the rhythm changes.

4/4 has four beats, 2/4 has two for each measure of music. Don't play fast, or speed up.

4/4

D///	D///	A7///	D///
D///	D///	A7///	D///
D///	D///	A7///	D///
D///	D///	A7///	D///

2/4

D/	A7/	D/	A7/
D/	A7/	D/	A7/
D/	A7/	D/	A7/
D/	A7/	D/	A7/

The changes are coming faster.

If you are having trouble making the changes, slow down.

You can do it!

4/4   **2/4**

D/A7/	D/A7/	D/	A7
D/A7/	D/A7/	D/	A7
D/A7/	D/A7/	D/	A7
D/A7/	D/A7/	D/	A7

4/4

D///	A7///	D/A7/ D///
D///	A7///	D/A7/ D///
D///	A7///	D/A7/ D///
D///	A7///	D/A7/ D///

74

chords in the left hand. Next we added some musical spice by introducing right-hand strumming patterns. For the third course of our musical dinner, we are adding some rhythmic complexity to the main course.

All of these ingredients will be present in the playing of a fine guitarist. Even though your achievements to this point have been modest, you can now begin to understand the voyage on which you have embarked.

Remember if you are having trouble making the chord changes without stumbling, slow the tempo down until you can do it. Try counting out loud, or having someone else count for you.

3/4 time has three beats to a bar of music.

Keep it slow, but DON'T SLOW DOWN.

You should be catching on to the rhythm changes now.

4/4

D///	A.7///	D///	D///
D///	A.7///	D///	D///
D///	A.7///	D///	D///
D///	A.7///	D///	D///

3/4

D//	D//	A.7//	D//
D//	D//	A.7//	D//
D//	D//	A.7//	D//
D//	D//	A.7//	D//

The section below has more and more rhythm changes.

Remember each slash line, and each chord name gets one beat.

Next we're going to learn some details about reading music and tablature.

2/4   **3/4**

DA.7	DA.7	D//	D//
DA.7	DA.7	D//	D//
DA.7	DA.7	D//	D//
DA.7	DA.7	D//	D//

4/4

D//	A.7//	D///	D///
D//	A.7//	D///	D///
D//	A.7//	D///	D///
D//	A.7//	D///	D///

THE TABLATURE SYSTEM

Tablature is a system that enables a guitarist to read music without using musical notation

Before 1750 music for guitar and lute was written in tablature rather than stardard musical notation. In the tablature system, rather than using notes, the player is simply given the name of the string and the correct fret to finger with the left hand.

The obvious advantage of tablature is that the guitarist who uses it doesn't have to learn to read musical notation. It does not, however, solve the problem of notating the rhythm of a particular note.

Musical notation uses the same music staff that players of other instruments use. We'll get into that later, but the disadvantage is that the player needs to know how to read the notes on the staff, and then to translate that knowledge to the guitar.

TABLATURE STAFF

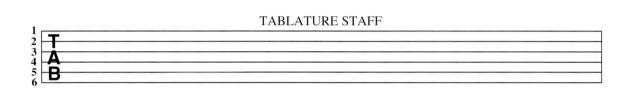

- The tablature staff has six lines. The 6th string is on the bottom (sixth line), the 5th string is on the fifth line, etc.

- The dots indicate where the left-hand fingers go. The number 2 means that your finger should be on the 2nd fret.

- A note on the bottom line that has a 3 on it means that you should finger the 6th string at the 3rd fret.

- Tablature, unlike musical notation does not use the spaces, only the lines. Remember, the numbers marked are the fret numbers. The lowest string is the lowest line of the tablature.

- To read the rhythms, look at the musical notation staff.

To put it in another way, the music staff is used by all musicians, and is no more relevant to the guitar than to the mandolin or the harmonica.

The advantage of tablature is that it omits that second step of the player having to translate notation to the instrument. The player can immediately make that adjustment. The tablature music staff has six lines, each line representing one string. The lowest line represents the 6th string, the next the fifth, and the highest line indicates the 1st string. The following diagrams illustrate the tablature staff.

The first staff shows the six-line tablature staff. The second staff indicates that the note to play is the 6th string at the 3rd fret. The third and fourth staffs indicate other notes to be played on various strings. These are all played on the accompanying audio tracks.

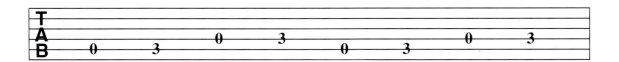

- Play 5th string open, then 5th string at the 3rd fret, 4th string open, 4th string at the 3rd fret, and repeat.

- The great thing about tablature is that if you can count, you can read it.

- Tablature was used for guitar and lute in the Middle Ages.

- Tablature can be used for any guitar tuning.

- By now you should understand the tablature system.

- Pete Seeger reintroduced tablature to guitar players.

- This time we'll skip around the strings. If you become confused, listen to track 9 of the audio tracks.

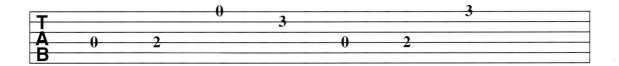

READING TABLATURE
There are two methods for reading tablature

Below are some additional examples of tablature. The first three examples are single notes in tablature. Tablature can also indicate two or three notes, or even entire chords.

There are two ways to deal with reading rhythms when you write tablature. One method is to use the same sort of musical figures that are found on the music staff—quarter notes, half notes, etc. These figures can be attached to the

individual notes indicated in the tablature.

The other method of indicating rhythms is to have the music line directly above the tablature line. When the guitarist needs to sort out the correct rhythms, he can simply look up at the line of music.

This is the practice I have followed later in this book when we get to songs. The music line is on top, and the tablature

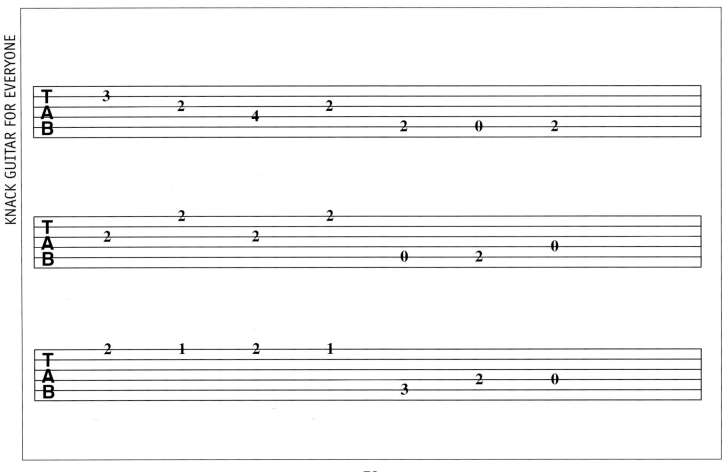

appears directly below it. It is fairly common for guitar players to use alternate tunings that often differ considerably from the usual guitar tuning. Even guitarists who are skilled at reading music often turn to tablature when the guitar is tuned differently. The reason for this is that the player who is reading from the music staff will have to keep telling himself that the notes indicated in the written music are not in the same place on the guitar that they would be if the guitar was tuned normally.

Ideally you will become comfortable with reading both music and tablature, and there are instances where either or both of them will come in handy.

- The tablature below indicates that you are playing two strings together. The notes are on the 3rd and 1st strings.

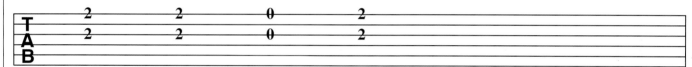

- Now we'll try some chords—three-note sequences.

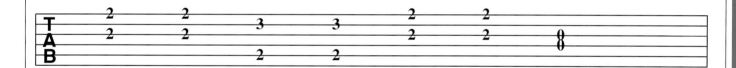

TABLATURE & MUSIC

READING MUSIC
Guitar music is written in the treble clef

Music notation can involve two musical staffs: the treble and the bass clefs. Guitar music is written on the treble clef, so guitar players need not learn to read the bass clef.

The notes of the treble clef are divided into four spaces and five lines. Reading from bottom to top: the spaces are the notes FACE. The lines are EBGDF. If you simply remember the word face, you will remember the names of the spaces.

To remember the names of the lines, the most common method is the saying "every good boy does fine."

The notes of the guitar in the typical tuning are: EADGBE. The lowest note on the guitar, unfortunately, is below the treble clef as it is drawn. To read the notes on the 6th and 5th strings of the guitar, you have to read lines and spaces that are below the normal image of the treble clef. We'll come

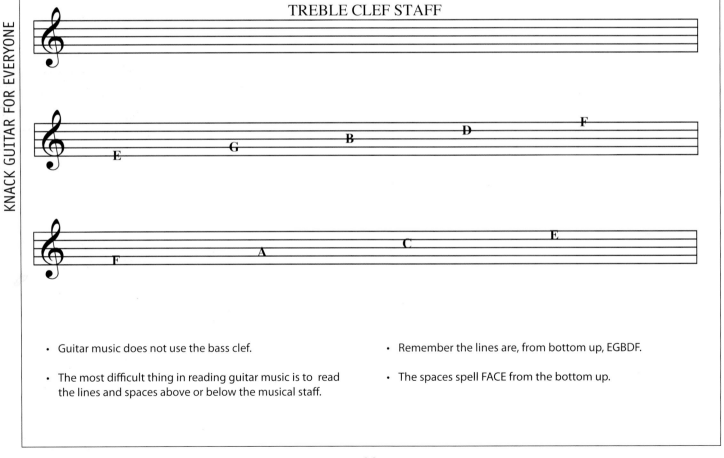

TREBLE CLEF STAFF

- Guitar music does not use the bass clef.

- The most difficult thing in reading guitar music is to read the lines and spaces above or below the musical staff.

- Remember the lines are, from bottom up, EGBDF.

- The spaces spell FACE from the bottom up.

back to that concept a little further on. For now, concentrate on learning the notes in the treble clef and the notes on the open strings of the guitar.

Just as there are notes below the treble clef, there are notes that are above the treble clef. When you begin to learn more advanced music that requires you to play up the neck of the guitar, you will be playing notes that are above the treble clef.

- The open strings on the guitar are, from bottom to top, EADGBE. They are shown in the music notation on a treble clef. The low E is the most difficult note to read, because it is four spaces below the staff.

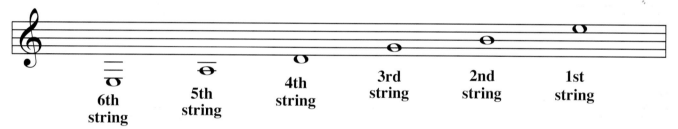

6th string 5th string 4th string 3rd string 2nd string 1st string

- The bass clef is used for low-pitched instruments like the string bass or bass trombone.

- Guitar music is not written in the bass clef.

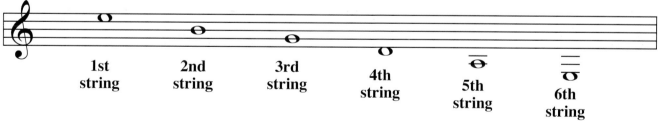

1st string 2nd string 3rd string 4th string 5th string 6th string

5th string open

81

NOTES ON THE GUITAR
We will now begin to relate the notes on the treble clef to the notes on the guitar

In addition to the notes that occur when the guitar strings are played open, when you fret the strings with your left hand you play other notes. For example, the 1st string played open is an E note. When you finger the 1st string at the 1st fret, it becomes an F note. It will take a while before you feel comfortable relating the notes of the guitar to the notes on the music staff. When you get to that point, you will be reading music for the guitar.

Below is a diagram, indicating the notes on the first four frets of the guitar.

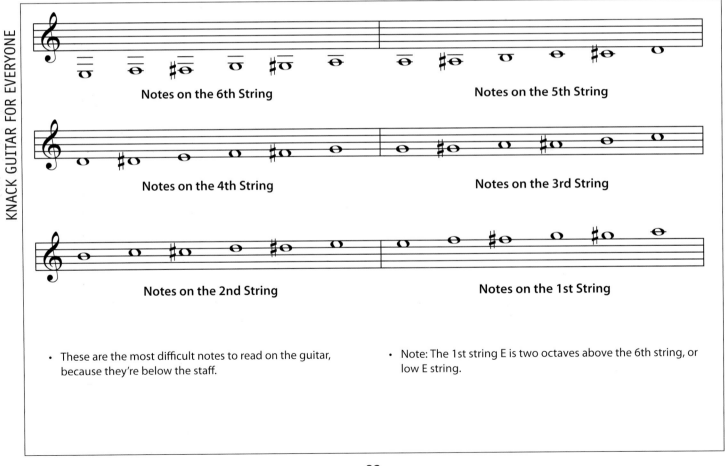

Notes on the 6th String

Notes on the 5th String

Notes on the 4th String

Notes on the 3rd String

Notes on the 2nd String

Notes on the 1st String

- These are the most difficult notes to read on the guitar, because they're below the staff.

- Note: The 1st string E is two octaves above the 6th string, or low E string.

6th string	5th string	4th string	3rd string	2nd string	1st string
E (open)	A	D	G	B	E
F (1st fret)	A♯	D♯	G♯	C	F
F♯ (2nd fret)	B	E	A	C♯	F♯
G (3rd fret)	C	F	A♯	D	G
G♯ (4th fret)	C♯	F♯	B	D♯	G♯

NOTES TO THE 5TH FRET

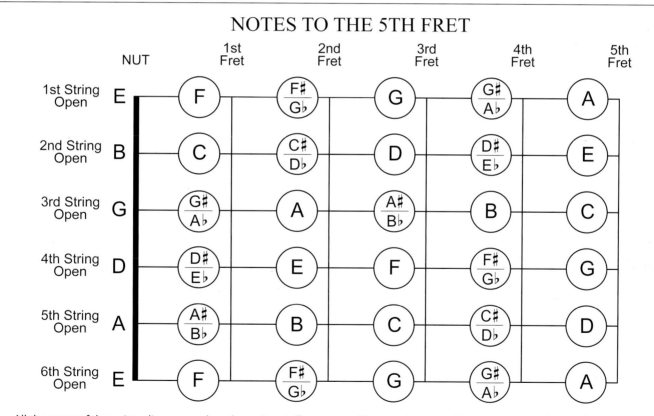

- All the notes of the guitar, diagrammed on the guitar staff.
- If you are interested in learning to read music for the guitar, you can use these notes as a reference.

RHYTHMS

In order to read music well, you must read rhythms as easily as you read notes

Immediately after the treble clef sign, you will notice a series of numbers, such as 4/4. This will be written with one number on top of the other as shown below. The number on top tells the player how many beats there are in each bar, or subdivision of music. The bottom number tells what a unit of time is in the piece. In other words, a bar that is marked 4/4

means that there are four quarter notes for each bar of music. 6/8 tells you that there are six eighth notes in the bar. Most music uses a consistent rhythm, so that if you see the 4/4 symbol, that will be the proper rhythm for the entire piece. Modern music is less predictable, and the Beatles, for example, were fond of throwing a bar or even an entire section of,

Dotted Notes

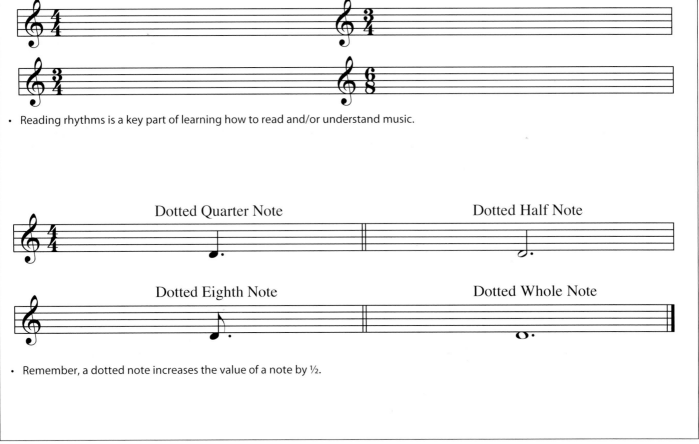

- Reading rhythms is a key part of learning how to read and/or understand music.

- Remember, a dotted note increases the value of a note by ½.

for example, 3/4, in what was basically a 4/4 tune.

The sort of notes that are commonly used are sixteenth notes, eighth notes, quarter notes, half notes, and whole notes. When a dot appears after a note, it increases the value of the note by a half. So a dotted quarter note in a 4/4 bar of music receives one and a half beats. Rests can be of any duration, but the most common are a quarter note, a half note, or a whole note long. A quarter note rest in 4/4 time is a one-beat rest, a half note rest in 4/4 lasts for two beats, and so forth.

ZOOM

Commercials often use odd numbers of bars, because the music has to follow the action, and the timing is very specific. I was once playing on a session in New York, and saw a flute player missed his entrance three. He turned to the composer, and said, "Mitch, I'm not used to playing any music in 4/4 time anymore."

4 Bars of Music, 4/4, 4/4, 3/4 and 4/4

- Remember a 4/4 bar of music contains four beats, a 3/4 bar contains three beats.

- Another example of four bars of music in different rhythms.

- Rests are places where the instrument does not play.

TABLATURE & MUSIC

CHORDS

You have already been playing chords in this book; now we'll explain what they are

Chords use at least three notes. Shortly we will be covering the key of C, and because that key has no sharps or flats, our discussion of chords will relate to the key of C. It applies equally to any other key, it's just that C is the easiest key to visualize.

The major scale in the key of C uses the following notes:

C D E F G A B C. A major chord uses the first, third and fifth notes of the scale. So a C major chord contains the notes C, E, and G. In folk, country, and blues songs, a very large percentage of the repertoire is playable using three chords. These chords are usually played on the first, fourth, and fifth notes of the scale. The scale is often thought of as being expressed

C Minor in Notation

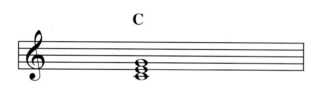

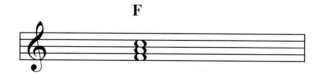

- The notes in C major are CEG, in C minor the notes are CE♭, G.

in roman numerals. In the key of C they are; II III IV V VI VII VIII or I (the next C scale repeats the sequence an octave higher.)

I II   III IV V VI VII I

C D   E F G A B C. D E F G A B C.

The F major chord uses the notes F A C.

The other thing that you need to know is that the chord played on the fifth note of the scale is usually, though not always, a seventh chord, one that requires an additional note. In the key of C this is the G7 chord, and the notes are G B D F. If you look at the list of notes on the left, the one with the roman numerals over the letters, and if you start with the G, by looking at the following list of notes, you will see that the fifth note of the chord is the D in the second sequence, and the seventh note is an F.

Minor chords take the third note of the chord and reduce it by a half step. The E becomes an E♭, so the notes are now C, E♭, and G.

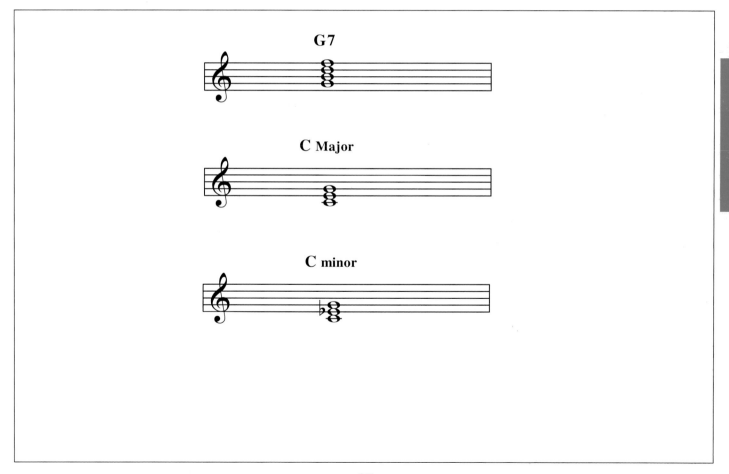

CHORD FINGERINGS
To prepare for our first song, make sure that your left-hand fingerings are accurate

After our short exploration into music theory, let's briefly review your left-hand fingering patterns.

By now, you should be able to move freely between the D and A7 chords without looking at the guitar.

You should be getting a good sound on your guitar, with the strings sounding clear, not muddy. We've provided some photos to illustrate some poor left-hand positions that may be preventing you from getting a good sound.

Here is a short checklist to use before takeoff:

Is the guitar playable, that is, can you play it for at least a half hour without having sore hands?

Are you using the right sort of strings for your guitar, and

Poor Fingering of D Chord in LH

- Remember, to finger a chord properly you must arch your wrist, establish a relaxed position of the left thumb, and make sure your left-hand fingers do not overlap one another.

- I am assuming your guitar is playable, and has no severe problems.

- Don't play the 6th string with the D chord.

Poor Fingering of A7 Chord

- You should not be having any problems with the A7 chord by now.

- Remember, you can play all six strings with the A7 chord.

- Still looking at the guitar when you change chords?

for the strength of your hand? (More on strings later in this chapter.)

Do the strings sound dull to you? If so, it's probably time to change them. Are you practicing on a regular, daily basis?

Remember, twenty minutes a day, six days a week, is better than playing one day a week for two hours.

Changing from D to A7

- Begin by practicing slowly.

- Next, speed the tempo up.

- Play with your fingers for a while, then use the pick.

- Keep one rhythm steady.

Changing from A7 to D

- Later in this chapter you will play your first song.

- You should be equally capable of playing with your right thumb or with a pick.

- Don't slow down when you change the chord.

STRING THICKNESSES

There are many types of guitar strings available; this will help you understand your options

Because of the great popularity of the guitar, there are dozens of different string types available for the instrument. The two basic considerations involved are the thickness of the string and the type of material that the string is made of. The thickness of the string is partly dictated by the size of your guitar. If you are playing a very small guitar and you put

heavy gauge strings on it, the strings will probably buzz horribly, and the guitar neck may even warp because it is not made to withstand this amount of pressure. If you are playing a very large-bodied guitar, like a dreadnought-size instrument, extra light strings will sound very thin, and they may buzz as well. Nowadays the gauge of strings varies from the

KNACK GUITAR FOR EVERYONE

Extra Light Gauge String

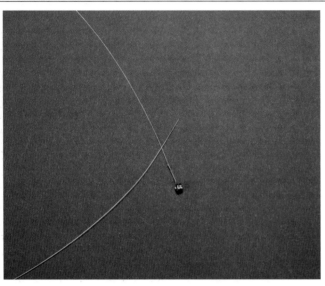

- Extra light gauge strings are easy on the left hand.

- Extra light strings don't produce a lot of volume.

- The gauge of strings you use is a blend of your own musical taste, your technical abilities, and your sound preferences.

Light Gauge String

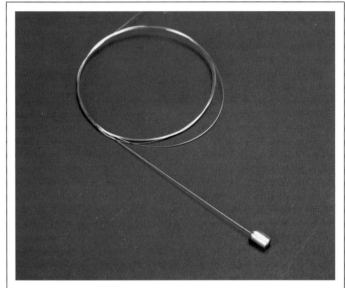

- Many players favor light gauge strings, because they are playable and also sound good.

- If you become exceptionally picky about your strings, you can buy sets that are made to order.

- This enables you to use the gauge for each string that you may prefer. Any music store has light or medium gauge strings available.

so-called "super slinky" strings favored by hard rock players, to extra light gauge strings, favored by some fingerpickers, to light gauge, medium, and heavy gauge strings. There are even gauges of string that represent a compromise between the gauges of, for example, light and medium gauge strings. Light and extra light gauge strings are best for beginners, because they don't require the left hand to exert much pressure in fingering the chords.

In addition to the issue of the string gauge, there is the question of what material the strings contain. Steel strings can be made of more or less copper and zinc, and the company that makes Gore-Tex coats its strings with a poly-web material that is supposedly designed to last longer (and which costs more to buy).

Medium Gauge String

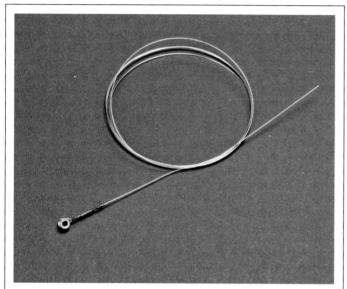

- If you have a larger-body guitar, you may prefer to use medium gauge strings.

- Another reason to use them is because they sound louder than light gauge strings do.

- Some guitars will buzz if you use the wrong gauge of string on them.

Heavy Gauge String

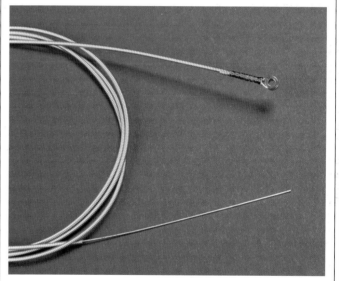

- Heavy gauge strings are not used by too many guitarists. People with exceptionally strong and large hands may prefer them.

- Never use a heavy gauge string on a small-bodied guitar. They could damage the top.

- You may find that as you become a more experienced player you will change the gauge of string that you use on your guitar.

STRINGS OF DIFFERENT MATERIALS

We will complete our discussion of strings in this section

Classical and flamenco guitarists use nylon strings. The strings that are marked with the words "high tension" tend to be brighter. They are favored by flamenco guitarists and classical guitarists who are looking for a louder, brighter sound. Guitarists looking for a sweeter sound will want to avoid high tension strings.

Electric guitar strings differ according to the style of music that they will be used to play. Lead guitarists tend to favor extremely light gauge strings, while jazz guitarists tend to prefer a somewhat heavier gauge of string. Anyone using extremely light gauge strings should be prepared for the strings to break while they are being played. This is especially true for guitarists who either play very hard, or who continually bend the strings.

Nylon String

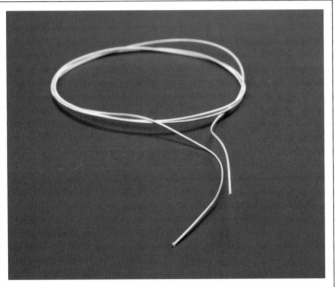

- Nylon strings are favored by classical and flamenco players.

- Nylon strings sound softer than steel strings.

- People who sing quiet ballads like nylon strings.

- Some of the Brazilian bossa nova guitarists use nylon strings.

Steel String

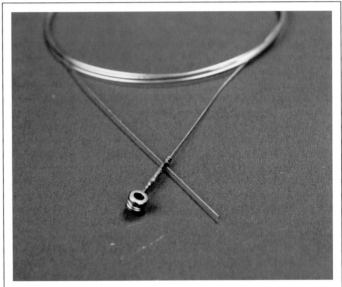

- Steel strings have a strong and somewhat jangly sound.

- Most rock, blues, and jazz guitarists use steel strings.

- Electric guitars use extremely light gauge steel strings.

Silk and steel strings are steel strings that use a thinner core in the bass strings. They are easier to finger, sound sweet as opposed to bright, and they tend to need changing more often. They are definitely easier on the left hand.

There are a few cautionary notes about strings. Classical guitarists should *never* put steel strings on a classical or flamenco guitar. Besides the fact that they will sound awful, these guitars are not braced to withstand the pressure of steel strings. Nylon strings will not hurt a steel-string guitar, but they will sound floppy and almost cartoonish.

One last note about strings. I generally change the bass strings on all of my guitars about twice as often as I change the treble strings. This is because I find that the sound of the bass notes seems to become dull, and I feel the need for a better defined bass. This is a matter of personal taste, as are many aspects of choosing strings. Although there are dozens of brands of strings, most of them are made by only a half dozen string manufacturers. Each brand has its adherents, so experiment with different brands.

Silk and Steel String

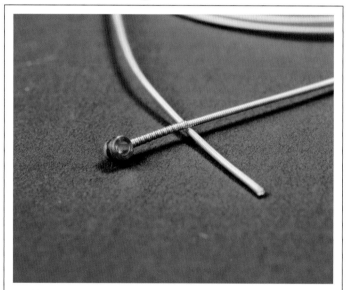

- Silk and steel strings are a sort of compromise between nylon and steel strings.

- Silk and steel strings are very easy on the left hand.

- Silk and steel strings are sometimes called compound strings.

Electric Rock Guitar String

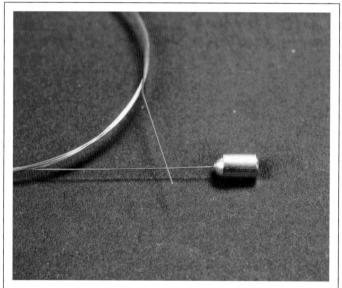

- These strings are sometimes referred to as "super slinky" strings.

- It is very easy to break these strings, because they are so thin.

- Electric blues players who bend their strings hard prefer these strings.

"SKIP TO MY LOU"

Here is our first song—included because it is easy to play

Below is the melody of "Skip to My Lou," in tablature and music. You may remember it from childhood days, or from singing it to your own children. The melody is also on the MP3, so even if you haven't heard it before, you will be able to hear it even without the music and tablature. I have also included the lyrics so you can sing it as well.

At this point, all of the time you have spent practicing chord changes should pay off. For now, don't worry about playing chords, even though they are shown above. Notice that the song is in 4/4 time, which means that there are four beats for each measure of music. To help you read the music or tab, a quarter note gets one beat, and an eighth note gets a half a

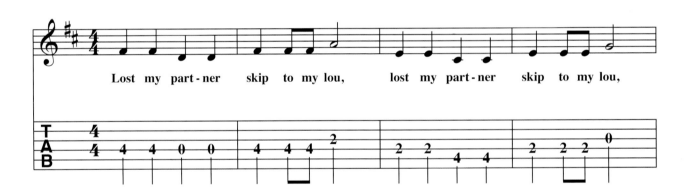

SKIP TO MY LOU

Lost my part-ner skip to my lou, lost my part-ner skip to my lou,

- You can follow this melody in either music or tab.

- Try using both systems.

- First you learn to play the melody, and then we will add a right-hand strum.

- The melody to the verse and chorus are quite similar, but not identical.

- First, try playing the melody using the right thumb only.

- Next, alternate the melody between the thumb and first finger.

beat. The half notes get two beats each. So, for example, the first bar of the chorus, the one that says "skip to my Lou," is counted as follows:

Skip to my Lou
1   and a 2

In many ways the most difficult aspect of reading music is playing rhythms, not the notes. So don't worry if this seems

a little confusing to you. Don't hesitate to refer to the audio track.

Also pay attention to variations in the melody; in this song, the verse and the chorus are quite similar, but not identical.

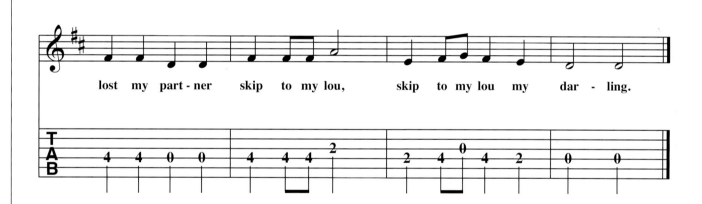

lost   my part - ner   skip   to my lou,   skip   to my lou   my   dar - ling.

- Now play the melody with the pick, picking down.

- Next play the melody with the pick picking up, or toward your body.

- Try playing the melody with alternating up and down picks.

- Try playing the melody with a thumb pick.

- Now try the melody with a thumb pick and a fingerpick.

- Alternate the notes.

- Finally, try the melody using any right-hand technique that you choose.

"SKIP TO MY LOU," PART II

In the previous spread you learned the melody; now we'll add a right-hand strum

The guitar is a wonderful instrument because it can be used not only for playing melodies, but also for adding strums to the melody, making songs come to life. At this point you will simply sing the melody. The guitar is only playing chords. Later on you will be able to integrate melodies into your playing, but for now it is best to play the strum on the guitar, make the chord changes as shown, and sing or hum the melody.

For the strum, we are going to use the same simple strum that you used when you were practicing changing from D to A7. Brush down across the strings, either with your right thumb, or with a flat pick. Remember to avoid the 6th string when you are playing the D chord. The reason is simple; it is

D
T   T T T   T   T T T
Lost my partner, what'll I do?
A7
T   T T T   T   T T T
Lost my partner, what'll I do?
D
T   T T T   T   T T T
Lost my partner, what'll I do?
A7   D
T   T   T   T T T T   T
Skip to my Lou, my darling.

- Strum across the strings with your thumb.

- Remember, don't play the 6th string with the D chord.

- Don't worry about the rhythm, for now.

Additional verses
D
I'll get another one, prettier than you,
D
I'll get another one, prettier than you,
D
I'll get another one, prettier than you,
A7   D
Skip to my Lou, my darling.

Flies in the buttermilk, what'll I do?
Flies in the buttermilk, what'll I do?
Flies in the buttermilk, what'll I do?
Skip to my Lou, my darling.

- Try the same thing, with some other verses.

- In the third verse see if you can hear the correct place to change the chord.

- If you can't hear the place where the chord changes, consult the verse above.

- Try the new verses using the right thumb in the same way.

the note E, which is not in the D chord. On the A7 chord, you can play all of the strings.

To make things as simple as possible, we have printed the words and the names of the correct chord with the strum directly over the words. Below, we have printed the chorus twice, using a new strum for the second chorus. In this strum the thumb will alternate between picking the strings down (from the lowest to the highest note, and back). We have marked the strum as TD (thumb down) and TU (thumb up).

Chorus #1

```
D
T    T   T        T
Skip, skip, skip to my Lou,
A7
T    T   T        T
Skip, skip skip to my Lou,
D
T    T   T        T
Skip, skip skip to my Lou,
A7                 D
T        T   T T
Skip to my Lou, my darling.
```

Chorus #2

```
D
T D T U T    D    D U
Skip, skip, skip to my Lou,
A7
T D T U T    D    T U
Skip, skip, skip to my Lou, D
T D T U T    D    D U
Skip, skip, skip to my Lou,
A7              D
T   D    T  U T D T U
Skip to my Lou, my darling
```

THE SIMPLE G CHORD

Once you have learned your third chord, you will be able to play hundreds of songs

This section will introduce the simple G chord. In this version of the G, don't play the 6th and 5th strings, because these notes are not in the chord. Your challenge now is to be able to play all three chords, D, G, and A7, without having to struggle to find the proper left-hand fingerings.

Try the following sequences, picking down across the strings with your thumb or a flat pick. Remember each chord name or slash indicates a strum.

One Finger G Chord

- This is a simple version of the G chord.

- Your left ring finger fingers the note on the 1st string at the 3rd fret.

- Don't play the 6th or 5th strings with this version of the G chord.

- Try changing the chords from D, to simple G, to A7, to D.

Full G Chord

- This is the most difficult chord you have had yet. The left hand stretch is considerable to play this chord. The little finger of the left hand plays the 1st string at the 3rd fret, the ring finger plays the 6th string at the 3rd fret, and the middle finger plays the 5th string at the 2nd fret.

- Practice playing D to full G to A7 to D, very slowly.

4/4	D///	D///	G///	G///
	D///	D///	A7///	D///

Note: The full G is given only for reference here; don't practice it yet.

Next try:

4/4	D///	D///	A7///	A7///
	G///	G///	D///	D///

Full G Chord, Showing Bad Hand Position

- You may have trouble making the stretch to play this chord.

- Be careful to keep the little finger of the left hand arched.

- Practice the chord changes slowly.

Full G, Showing the LH Stretch Required

- Notice the arch of the wrist.

- Be sure that the 6th and 5th strings are not overlapping.

- This can easily happen, because of the stretch.

- Changing to and from the G chord is difficult.

CHORD CHANGES
Practicing chord changes with the full G chord

If you are able to master the art of changing from D to G to A7, you will now be able to play hundreds of songs. Because the full G chord involves something of a stretch, in the last chapter I suggested that you start with changing to the simplified version of G. With the full G chord you will be able to play all six strings of the guitar. It is therefore important that you begin to practice changing from D to G to A7, using the full G chord. With the full G chord at your fingertips, only on the D chord is there a string that you need to omit (the 6th and lowest string).

Practice the following chord changes:

4/4	D///	D///	G///	G///
	D///	D///	A7///	D///

D Chord

- There isn't much new to say about the D chord. You should know it backwards and forwards by now.

- Your next step will be changing from D to G.

- It's important to mentally anticipate a chord change before it actually occurs.

D Chord Going to One Finger G

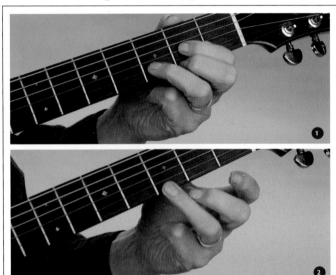

- Changing from D to simple G requires you to flip your wrist around slightly.

- Don't use superfluous motion in the left hand.

- Be ready to land on the G chord.

Next try:

2/4	D	D/	D/	D/
	A7/	A7/	G/	D/

D Chord Going to Full G

- To play the full G chord, you do have to turn your wrist around.

- Where is your left thumb?

- What is your wrist feeling like?

G Chord Going to A7

- To go to A7 you have to turn your wrist back around.

- It's not difficult to go from G to A7, because A7 is such an easy chord to play.

- Practice going back and forth between these chords.

FIRST THREE-CHORD SONG

MORE CHORD PRACTICE

It is of utmost importance that you become used to changing D-G-A7 in any sequence

The more time you spend practicing changing from D to G to A7 and back, in any sequence, the better prepared you will be to play songs. Check the following:

Are you keeping time? In other words do you have to slow down when you change the chords?

If this is happening, slow down your strum. It is very important to continue to develop muscle memory, so that you can change the chords without slowing down.

Are you getting a decent sound no matter what chord you are playing? If you are not hearing some notes in one of the chords, spend more time going back and forth to that chord than to the other ones.

A7 Chord Going to D

- Remember that in 3/4 time you only play three beats per measure.

- If you're still having trouble with the full G chord, play the simple G.

- Whichever chord change is giving you the most trouble is the one you should practice the most.

D Chord Changing to Full G

- Different songs will require you to play different chord sequences. Moving to the G will probably slow you down at first.

- Remember, don't practice any faster than the time it takes you to make your most difficult chord change.

Is there a particular chord change that bothers you? Are you equally capable of going from D to G to A7 to G to A7 to D, etc.? Again, if one of these patterns bothers you, then spend more time practicing that chord change, rather than the other ones. Try the following:

3/4	D//	G//	G//	A7//
	G//	D//	A7//	D//
	A7//	A7//	G//	G//
	A7//	A7//	G//	D//

Full G Chord Going to D

- Don't rush!

- The G to D change may annoy you, because both chords use three fingers of the left hand.

- Remember to always be aware of the positions of your left wrist and thumb.

D Chord, Going to G, then A7

- Once you are able to make these chord changes without slowing down, you will have opened the door to playing hundreds of songs.

- The trick is to not play too fast. If you find yourself losing the rhythm, start over and slow down.

THE THUMB-INDEX STRUM

It's time to expand our strum vocabulary

Up until now, we have played everything with the thumb, or when we used the flat pick, it simply duplicated the actions of the thumb. Here we will begin to expand our use of strums by alternating single notes and strums. The right-thumb strums will play single notes on the bass strings (6th, 5th, or 4th strings), and the index finger will brush down across the strings. The sequence will go like this:

1) Thumb plays bass string.
2) Index finger brushes down across strings.

You should play the strum evenly, with each step taking up a quarter note. When you brush down across the strings, be sure to play the three highest strings (3rd, 2nd, and 1st), and you can also play the 4th string. The main intention of this

RH Thumb Plays Bass Note

- This strum alternates a single bass note, played by the thumb, with a downward brush by the index finger.

- Keep the rhythm even; you can also try this wearing a thumb pick.

Right Index Finger Brushes Down

- The index finger brushes down across the highest four strings.

- This is a very basic strum, yet it has been used on many recordings.

- The thumb and index notes are even.

strum is to contrast the bass note, played with the thumb, with the chord, played by the index finger.

Now try the same strum with a flat pick. First pick one of the bass strings, then brush down across the strings with the pick. The sequence is:

1) Play bass string with the flat pick.
2) Brush down across the higher strings with the pick.

As with the finger-style strum, the rhythm is even: Each part of the strum is a quarter note.

Pick Plays Bass Note

- Use a flat pick to pick a bass note.

- You will be picking down with the pick.

- When you first use a pick, you sometimes don't hit the note that you're aiming at.

Pick Brushes Down

- Strum down with the pick across the highest four strings.

- You should hit the bass note fairly hard, so that the strum doesn't overshadow the bass note.

- Notice that the sound of the pick is different than when executing the strum with your fingers. They each have their uses.

ANOTHER STRUM
We will now expand on the strum shown in the last section

The more strums that you add to your repertoire, the more fun you will have playing the guitar, and the better your playing will sound. The strum that we will cover in this section is a logical extension of the one in the last spread. You still will be using the thumb and the index finger, but now the index finger will be picking back, as well as down. Here is the sequence:

Thumb plays a bass note, index finger brushes down across the strings, index finger brushes *back* across the strings. The rhythm is a bit different: quarter note, followed by two eighth notes, or 1, 2+.

Notice how even a small change like this adds a considerable amount of color to your playing. Next practice using this strum with the chord changes. Then go back to "Skip to My

Right Thumb Picks Bass

- The thumb will play the bass note, as it did in the last strum.

- This time the thumb note is twice as long as the index

- strums. So the rhythm is 1, 2 and.

- Be sure that the bass note is clear.

Right Index Finger Brushes Down

- This is the same index brush stroke that we used in the last strum.

- The difference is that it is only half as long.

- Prepare to use the index finger to strum back.

Lou" and try this strum with it. Remember, the rhythm is long, short, short, or quarter note, eighth note, eighth note.

Practice going from one chord to another using this strum. Have a friend call out the chord names, and when they name a chord, you need to change to it. Do everything that you can to make playing the strum with the chord second nature to you.

Right Index Finger Brushes Back

- Brushing back is more awkward than brushing down.

- Remember the rhythm; the two brushes together have the same time value as the bass note.

- The addition of the double brush makes the strum much more lively.

Right Thumb Ready to Start Next Strum

- The thumb is now ready to play the next bass note.

- The next thumb note will be on a higher bass strum.

- On the G and A7 chords, the first thumb note is often the 6th string, followed by the thumb playing the 4th string. For the D chord the bass notes are the 5th string followed by the 4th string.

FIRST THREE-CHORD SONG

PICK-STYLE DOUBLE STRUM

We will now adapt the thumb double brush strum for the flat pick

The strum in this section is exactly the same as the previous strum, except that now you will be using a flat pick. Strumming up, or toward you with a flat pick, is more awkward than strumming down. You have to bend your wrist and elbow to pick back. You may also find that you tend to pick back across fewer strings than you did when you picked down. That isn't really a problem, as long as you hit at least two or three of the strings. You need to do that in order to differentiate the strum from the single bass note that you picked in step 1.

The sequence is now:
1) Flat pick play a single bass note (picking down).
2) Flat pick brushes down with the pick across three or four high strings.

Pick Plays a Bass Note

- The same strum can be executed with a flat pick.

- Remember to play the low bass note as the first part of the strum.

- After you hit the bass note, come to rest on the next highest string.

Pick Brushes Down

- Brush down with the pick across the top four strings.

- Be sure you have a firm grip on the pick.

- Prepare to brush back with the pick.

3) Flat pick brushes back across two or three strings. Once again, the rhythm is quarter note, eighth note, eighth note, or long, short, short.

If you have a thumb pick that has a blade like a flat pick, you might try doing the strum with the thumb pick, picking the single bass note, playing down with the thumb pick, and then back. Vary the strum by using the thumb pick and strumming, either with the index finger or with a fingerpick. Every one of these variations creates something of a different sound.

Pick Brushes Back

- The pick now brushes back across the strings.

- Because the motion of the pick is a sort of upward curl,

  it is a bit more awkward than the down strum.

- The pick ends up in the air, ready to:

Pick Ready to Start Again

- Come to rest on the next bass note.

- Remember the rhythm is 1, 2+, with the single note equal to the two strums.

- Up pick strums take some time to get used to.

109

THE "CRAWDAD SONG"
Our first three-chord song is the "Crawdad Song"

First we will learn the melody of the "Crawdad Song," and then we will adapt the strums that you learned in this chapter to the song. This will be the first song that we have encountered that actually uses three chords. The challenge is to make all the chord changes in rhythm, execute the strums, and also to sing or hum the melody. The tune is printed below in notation and tablature, but when you get to the pages that show the strums, don't worry about integrating the melody with the strum. That's a task for later on, when you've been playing for a while. Trying to anticipate some of the problems you may have playing this song:

Beware of the G chord. It is a bit harder to play than anything

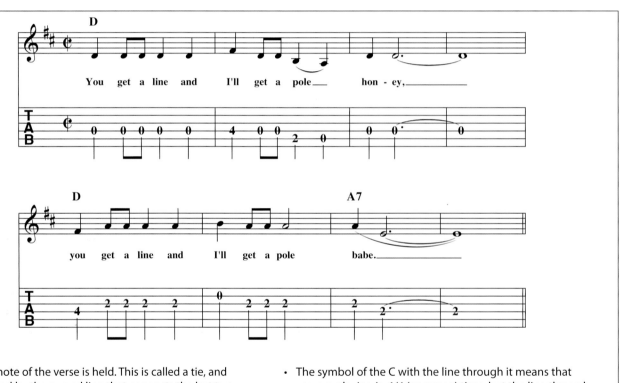

- The last note of the verse is held. This is called a tie, and is indicated by the curved line that connects the last two notes of the verse.

- The symbol of the C with the line through it means that you are playing in 4/4 (common) time, but the line through the C indicates that the song feels as though it were in 2, because it is played at a quick tempo.

you've attempted so far. Don't play too fast. If you do, you will probably get mixed up between executing the strum and changing the chords.

Once you are able to play this tune without hesitation, you might consider buying a songbook that includes guitar chords. You can then extend the knowledge that you are acquiring here to other songs. You'll have more fun, and you can increase your repertoire. You're almost ready to take the next step of playing with other people.

ZOOM

Check out your local music store for a fake book. Fake books are collections of songs, usually numbering in the hundreds in a particular style, such as country, blues, jazz, and so forth. They include the melodies of the songs along with chords. Stay away from jazz for now, because the chords are too demanding.

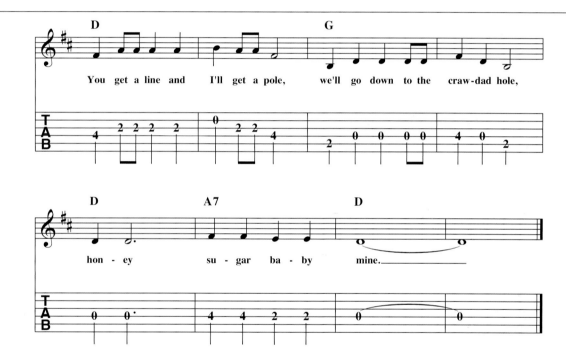

- The thumb and the index should be played evenly.
- Don't rush.
- Use the single brush strum.
- Now try it with the double strum.

- Remember the index strums are executed quickly.
- Don't worry about trying to play the melody on the guitar.
- Sing or hum as you play.

FIRST THREE-CHORD SONG

THUMB & 3 FINGERS, TOGETHER
We will now use the thumb and three fingers of the right hand

You probably have been wondering if you will ever get to use your other right-hand fingers to play the guitar. The time has come! The right index finger will be playing the 3rd string, picking up, or toward you, the middle finger will be playing the 2nd string, also picking up, and the ring finger will be playing the 1st string, picking toward you. The three fingers will be playing together. The sequence of the strum is:

1) Thumb plays a bass note.

2) Index finger picks up on the 3rd string, middle finger picks up on the 2nd string, and the ring finger picks up on the 1st string (together).

The rhythm is two even quarter notes.

Some people find that it is a little awkward to use the ring finger, but this is not a very demanding strum, so it shouldn't

Right Thumb Plays Low Bass Note

- The first bass note played is either the 6th or the 5th string, depending upon which chord is being played.

- Remember that the 6th string cannot be played with the D chord.

- The thumb will be playing again after you play the next step of the strum.

1st, 2nd, and 3rd Fingers of RH Play Together

- The three fingers of the right hand are picking up, or toward you.

- Each right-hand finger should play only the note that it is playing.

- To avoid playing superfluous strings, or making your sound "cloudy," don't play too hard.

give you much trouble. The sound that you are looking for is a more mellow sound than you got when you were using the thumb and index strum in the last chapter.

Right Thumb Plays Higher Bass Note

- The thumb now plays the 4th string.

- You can also experiment with having the thumb play the 5th string, when the first bass note is on the 6th string.

- You should bend the thumb back after you play, so that it is ready to play the lower bass note again.

1st, 2nd, and 3rd Fingers of RH Play Together

- This is the same strum used in step two.

- In order to prepare for this strum you will need to have lifted the three fingers up

off the strings, in preparation to use them again.

- The thumb and three fingers should be ready to start the strum again.

THUMB & 3 FINGERS, INDIVIDUALLY

Now take the same three fingers, and have them play individual notes

Although the strum that was introduced in the last spread is a good contribution to helping you develop more facility in the right hand, using the same three fingers to pick the notes individually is a technique used by many professional guitarists. The sequence is:

1) Thumb plays bass note.

2) Index finger picks up on 3rd string.

3) Middle finger picks up on 2nd string.

4) Ring finger picks up on 1st string.

The notes are four even eighth notes. Try to play each note as cleanly as possible. Even if you were able to use the ring finger easily in the last section, you may have some trouble

Right Thumb Plays Bass Note

- Thumb plays only one note.
- Thumb comes to rest on string.

Index Finger Plays 3rd String

- Index finger curls up after hitting each string.
- Prepare to use the right-hand middle finger.

here. This classic strum is called the arpeggio, and it sounds particularly good on nylon-string guitars.

Try to play the chord changes using this arpeggio. For example, play:

D   G   D   A7   D .

Use a full arpeggio on each chord.

As is the case with each new strum you learn, you may experience some problems coordinating the chord changes with the arpeggio strum.

Another enjoyable experiment is to combine both of the

strums with the thumb and three fingers, playing alternately together and separately. This sequence will be:

1) Thumb plays bass.
2) Three fingers together
3) Thumb plays higher bass note.
4) Index finger plays 3rd string.
5) Middle finger plays 2nd string.
6) Ring finger plays 1st string.

The rhythm here is quarter note, quarter note, followed by four eighth notes.

Middle Finger of RH Plays 2nd String

- Middle finger curls up after hitting the 2nd string.
- Prepare to use the right-hand ring finger.

3rd Finger of RH Plays 1st String

- The right ring finger may seem awkward at first.
- Right-hand little finger is held, in the air. Be ready to start to strum again.

LEARNING A MELODY
"The Banks of the Ohio"

One of the classic genres of American folk songs is the murder ballad. The murder is often brought about by a woman not doing whatever her male companion has requested, or because in his opinion, the woman has been unfaithful to him. Folksinger Joan Baez brought this old murder ballad to a new audience. Try to match the lyric with your guitar tone. If you play near the bridge of the guitar, you will get a harsher sound.

When the lyrics dictate it, move your right hand to the top of the guitar neck to get a softer, more mellow sound. If you play directly over the sound hole of the guitar, you will get the most rounded sound.

For those reading the music, notice that there are many

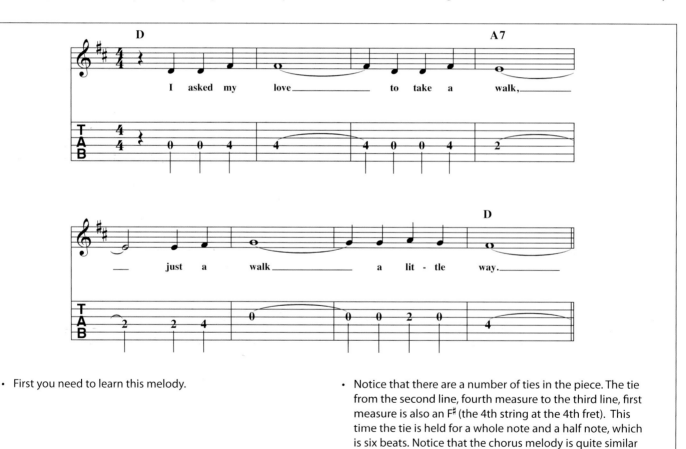

- First you need to learn this melody.

- Notice that there are a number of ties in the piece. The tie from the second line, fourth measure to the third line, first measure is also an F♯ (the 4th string at the 4th fret). This time the tie is held for a whole note and a half note, which is six beats. Notice that the chorus melody is quite similar to the verse melody, but not identical with it. This occurs in many songs.

low D notes in this song. D is the first space below the treble clef. Between the second and the third measures, you will notice a line connecting the note (F#, or the 4th string at the 4th fret). This is called a tie. The tie is a held note, in other words you continue to hold the note, but you do not play it again. Notice that the song does not begin on the first beat of the measure, but on the second beat. The three notes at the beginning are called "pick-up notes."

You will also notice that the song ends on the first beat of the measure. Since the piece is in 4/4 time, the total number of beats needs to come out even.

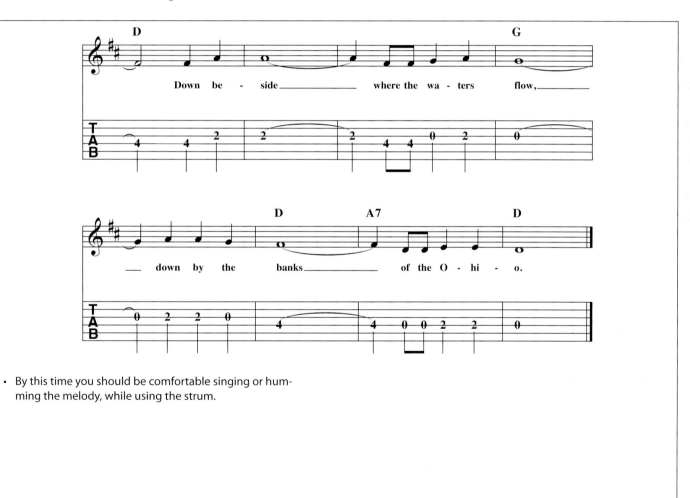

- By this time you should be comfortable singing or humming the melody, while using the strum.

RIGHT-HAND ARPEGGIOS

The arpeggio requires the use of the thumb and three right-hand fingers.

In order to master this strum, it is important that each note be very clear.

The only note that you should be able to hear is the single string that you are playing.

In order to use your right-hand ring finger, you need to arch your right wrist. Most people find using the ring finger

a bit awkward, because it is not a finger that you use regularly when you move your hand. If you think about the way the guitar is laid out, remember that usually the thumb is assigned to play bass notes, while the first three fingers of the right hand play the 3rd, 2nd, and 1st strings. Practice doing this, even without playing a chord. Can you hear each note

Right Thumb Plays 6th String

- Note: The number 3 means the three fingers should be playing together, T means the thumb plays. Because the melody begins on the second beat of the measure, don't start the strum until you get to the word "love." Brush once across the strings at the beginning of the song, and start the

strum on the word "love."

- Note: play one brush stroke across the strings before starting the strum.

- Notice that in the arrangement of the verse we use the thumb and the three fingers together to strum.

Right Thumb Plays 4th String

- Are you varying your sound by moving the fingers of your right hand?

- Are you able to sing or hum while you are playing

without losing track of the rhythm?

- Can you play this strum without looking at your right hand?

clearly? Are you hearing only the single strings that you are picking, or are there extraneous notes audible because you don't have good control over each finger of your right hand? You may have to play harder with the ring finger, because you have less control over it.

Right Thumb Plays 5th String

- You have already used the thumb in this way several times.

- Are you ready to play the next thumb note?

- You will have to lift the right thumb slightly to play the next note.

Three Fingers Together

- You should be used to this by now.

- After you play the notes together, you will need to

- lift the hand so that you can play the rest of the strum.

- Are you playing too fast?

BACKWARDS ARPEGGIO

This is similar to the normal arpeggio, but the sequence of notes is reversed

By reversing the order of the right hand fingers, it is possible to create a new strum. We will start out with the thumb, but the second note will be played by the ring finger of the right hand.

The order of the notes will become:

1) Thumb plays low bass string.

2) Ring finger plays 1st string.
3) Middle finger plays 2nd string.
4) Index finger plays 3rd string.

For the next arpeggio, the thumb will play the higher bass string (5th or 4th string), and the other fingers will repeat their sequence.

Arpeggio Playing

- There are a number of secrets to playing good-sounding arpeggios. Here are a few of them:

1) You need to have finger-nails on the first three fingers of the right hand.

2) The fingernails need to be even with no sharp edges.

3) You need to arch your right wrist.

4) Experiment with moving your right hand. Generally speaking, arpeggios sound best when played right over the sound hole of the guitar.

5) If it wasn't a softer sound,

you can move your fingers to play at the top of the guitar neck.

6) If you want a brighter sound, play near the bridge of the guitar.

Once you get used to doing this, try the following steps:

1) Thumb plays low bass note.
2) Three fingers play together.
3) Thumb plays high bass note.
4) Ring finger plays 1st string.
5) Middle finger plays 2nd string.
6) Index finger plays 3rd string.

7) Be sure your strings are not too worn to produce a good sound. One telltale sign of old strings is rusty strings. Another occurs when the string lining begins to wear out, to the point where you can actually see the lining of the strings eroding.

8) Arpeggios sound best when played on nylon-string guitars, or steel-string guitars that use light or extra-light gauge strings.

9) Some larger body–size guitars have boomy bass strings, and it is difficult to get a nice even sound with the right hand fingers when you play these guitars.

10) Be careful to hit only one string with each finger.

THE FORWARD-BACKWARD ARPEGGIO
It is possible to play the entire arpeggio in a different order

So far you have learned to play some versions of the arpeggio. The first example used the thumb and the three fingers playing together, and in the second version each finger picked up on single notes.

There are many other variations of the arpeggio that you can use. This one uses the same fingers in a slightly different way.

1) Thumb plays low bass note.
2) Index finger picks up on 3rd string.
3) Middle finger picks up on 2nd string.
4) Ring finger picks up on 1st string.
5) Ring finger again picks up on 1st .
6) Middle finger picks up on 2nd string.
7) Index finger picks up on 3rd string.

Right Thumb Plays Low Bass String

- Once again, the thumb is going to play the lower bass string.

- Get ready for each finger to play separately.

- The next note will be played by the 3rd string.

Index Finger of RH Plays 3rd String

- Remember you are picking up: toward you.

- Keep the wrist arched.

- The right hand should feel relaxed.

8) Thumb plays higher bass note.

The rhythm should be even—eight eighth notes.
It may take you a while to remember that the second note of the strum is played by the ring finger, not by the index finger. Things to remember:

Keep the right hand arched.
Don't play too hard, the object is to get a good, clear sound.

Middle Finger of RH Plays 2nd String

- You are still picking up, or toward you.

- Are you playing with a combination of nail and flesh?

- After you play the string, lift your finger off it.

Ring Finger of RH Plays 1st String

- Keep your wrist up.

- Don't rest any part of the right hand on the guitar.

- Prepare for the next step.

MORE ARPEGGIOS
This section completes the full arpeggio

We left the last section in mid-strum, so to speak. This is the first half of the full arpeggio. Each note should be played as cleanly as possible, and you should be able to hear each note separately from the preceding note. This is the basic sound of the classical guitar. Be sure to play just over the sound hole of the guitar.

You should expect that the ring finger of the right hand will be a bit awkward to use. In due time the strum will become natural to you. Remember that the goal is to play every note evenly.

It is possible to vary the arpeggio fingering. For example, you can play the fifth note in the sequence as a bass note with your thumb, with the sixth note played by the ring finger. Try to make up your own strum.

Ring Finger of RH Plays 1st String

- This may seem a bit awkward at first, but it isn't particularly difficult.

- The reason for using different versions of arpeggios is simply to add color to your playing.

- If you didn't lift the ring finger off the 1st string in the last part of the strum, this will be especially awkward to play.

Middle Finger of RH Plays 2nd String

- Now you are playing the last strum backwards.

- Remember to move each finger off the string, once you have played it.

- This isn't as difficult as you thought it might be!

Another variation is to play thumb, index, thumb middle, thumb ring finger, thumb middle. You can also experiment with playing two notes together.

Index Finger of RH Plays 3rd String

- This will be followed by the last thumb note.

- Keep some separation between your right thumb and the other fingers. In other words, extend the thumb.

- Once you get the idea, practice a bit faster.

Right Thumb Plays Bass

- This completes the strum.

- Try some variations of your own. What happens if the three fingers play the 4th, 3rd, and 2nd strings, instead of the 3rd, 2nd, and 1st strings?

- To check on your ability to control the right hand, keep each part of the strum going for a while, instead of alternating the strums.

- Try slowing down, just before the end of the song, on the words "be my bride." This is called a *ritard,* and it is often used to help dramatize a song.

C, F, & G7 CHORDS

The key of C is a very popular key for almost every musical instrument

One of the advantages of playing in the key of C is that virtually every musician is comfortable with that key. It is a particularly simple key for piano players, because it has no sharps or flats. Country guitar players enjoy the key of C, and certain tunes, such as "Wildwood Flower," are just about always played in that key.

You will need to learn three new chords to play in the key of C—C, F, and G7. F is probably going to give you a bit of trouble, but I recommend patience.

The more chords and keys that you are able to play in, the more fun you will be able to have when playing the guitar. As we will see later, 1950s rock tunes are also often played in the

C Chord

- The C chord is possibly the single most common guitar chord.

- Be sure to arch your ring finger, so that it only plays the note it is fingering, the 5th string at the 3rd fret.

- Be sure your wrist is turned toward you, so that you can finger all of the necessary notes in the chord.

- Do not play the 6th string with the C chord.

F Chord

- The F chord is not an easy one. You must finger both the 1st and 2nd strings at the 1st fret. If you do not apply enough left-hand pressure, the notes will be muffled.

- The thumb should be placed behind the guitar neck and be only half visible.

- It is virtually impossible to play this chord if your left wrist is not arched.

key of C, with some simple additional chords.

At this point you may want to purchase a guitar chord book, so that you can start adding chords on your own. Some of these books are encyclopedic in scope, so find one that seems user-friendly, and doesn't contain 1,001 chords or more. It is even possible to find small, thin books that will fit in your guitar case.

As you begin to learn these new chords, think ahead in your playing, anticipating where the chord changes will appear.

F Chord, from Another Angle

- If you are having trouble with the F chord, play the 1st and 2nd strings alone, fingering them with the first finger of the left hand. Are you getting a clear sound? Are you pressing hard enough?

- Next add the note on the 3rd string at the 2nd fret. Is the sound still clear?

- When you have added the note on the 4th string, you have completed the chord.

- Do not play the 6th string with the F chord.

Easy G7 Chord

- You have already played the G chord, now play the G7.

- The difference between the two chords is that G7 adds the note F to the chord.

- If F is really giving you prob-lems, play the G7 chord in a simplified version, finger-ing only the note on the 1st string. If you use that fingering, you cannot play the open 6th or 5th strings, because these notes are not in the G7 chord.

TROUBLESHOOTING F
Here is some first aid for playing this chord

The position of your left wrist is critical for you in terms of both the F and G7 chords, and even to some extent with the C chord. It is easy to feel like an absolute klutz, with overlapping, dull-sounding strings, a very tired left wrist, and a feeling that you have little or no control over the sound that you are getting.

The purpose of this section is to offer you some emergency assistance that should help you to conquer the dreaded F chord.

For starters, ask someone who has been playing for a while to play an F chord on your guitar. There are two reasons for doing this. One is so that you can see and hear that it is indeed possible to get a good sound when playing that chord. The other reason is to check on the condition of your guitar. If the

KNACK GUITAR FOR EVERYONE

F Chord with Poor Position of Left Wrist

- Playing the F chord is apt to be problematic, but you will definitely need to arch your left wrist to get a good sound. How does it sound to you?

- The problem could be in your left wrist position, or in the amount of pressure you are applying to the 1st and 2nd strings.

Overlapping Strings with F Chord

- If your 1st finger is not flat, either the 1st or 2nd string is apt to sound muffled.

- Another possibility is that the middle or ring finger of your left hand is hitting some other string besides the one that it should be playing.

- If there are any problems with your guitar, they are apt to show up here. These include old strings, overly high guitar action, a warped neck, etc.

strings are old, if the neck needs some attention because the strings are set too high off the fingerboard, or if you simply have a poorly made instrument, this is the time to act.

MAKE IT EASY

One simple exercise that can be helpful is to squeeze a small sponge ball with your left hand. I have seen people doing this on a subway train in New York, on commuter buses in various parts of the country, and even in college classrooms. The purpose of this exercise is to develop more strength in your left hand.

Inadequate Pressure in LH on F Chord

- Notice that in the photo the ring and middle fingers of the left hand are, so to speak, all over the place, rather than fingering the strings that they are supposed to be playing.

- If your fingers overlap, you will get muffled notes.

- You may even get additional notes besides the ones you are intending to finger.

3rd and 2nd Finger of LH Interfering

- If you are holding the 2nd and 3rd fingers too close together, they will very likely interfere with each other.

- The middle finger can easily interfere with the 1st finger as well.

- Is your wrist tired? If so, you may be applying more pressure than is necessary.

PRACTICING THE CHANGES
Let's put C, F, and G7 to use

Let's get to work and practice changing the chords that you've just learned. Once you get comfortable with these chords, we'll introduce another song.

If you look at the chord diagrams for the three chords, you can see that the changes in C require more left-hand movement than you experienced when you were playing the chords in the key of D. Run through C, F, and G7 as follows:

C///   C///   F///   F///
G7///   G7/// C///   C///

C///   C///   F///   F///
G7///   G7/// C///   C///

C///   C///   F///   F///

C Chord

- To move from C to F, you will need to move your left hand to the left, in a sort of pivoting motion.

- Can you hear every note in the C chord?

- Remember not to play the 6th string.

F Chord

- Be sure that you are solidly planted on the F chord.

- Your first finger should be flattened down on the 1st and 2nd strings, and you need to exert enough pres-

sure to make the notes ring out clearly. Remember, this is the hardest chord you've had yet.

- Remember not to play the 6th string.

G7///   G7/// C///   C///

C///   C///   F///   F///
G7///   G7/// C///   C///

Start off slowly, and don't increase your speed until you can change the chords without any pauses. If you can't tell whether these pauses are occurring because you're too busy looking for the correct hand positions, try recording yourself playing the chords. Tapping your foot may be helpful too.

G7 Chord

- The G7 chord requires quite a stretch, especially between the first and second fingers of the left hand.

- Be sure that the 6th and 5th strings, fingered by the ring and middle fingers of the left hand, are not overlapping.

- The left wrist should be arched.

- You can play the 6th string with this chord.

C Chord

- Each finger has to move up or down one string from the G7 chord, in order to make this change.

- Don't play the 6th string.

- The left wrist should also move slightly when you are making the chord change.

"KUMBAYA"
Try this old hymn with the new chords

"Kumbaya" is an old African hymn that is still widely sung. The next two pages contain the melody and the tablature.

When playing "Kumbaya," the main approach is to play rhythmically. This is a great singalong, and you should sing it with other people participating. When you sing along with others, keeping good time becomes absolutely essential.

There are many recordings of this song by such folk singers as Pete Seeger. You may want to find one of these recordings and sing along with the singer.

When you listen to professionals, notice how effortlessly they seem to make chord changes.

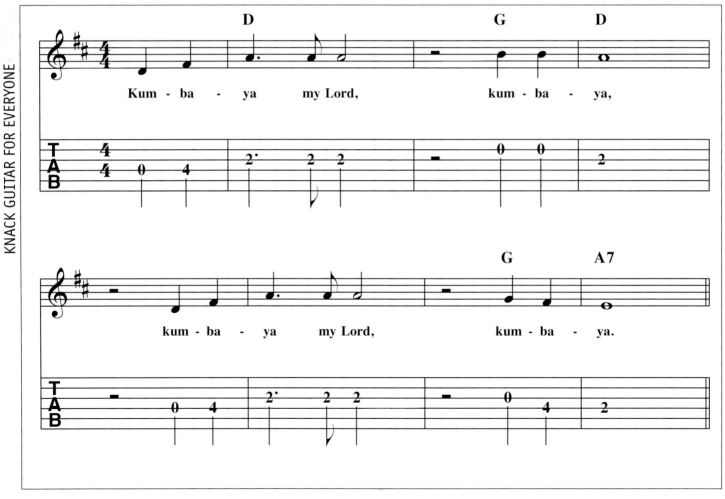

You should also try to play along with other guitarists. It is good practice and great fun.

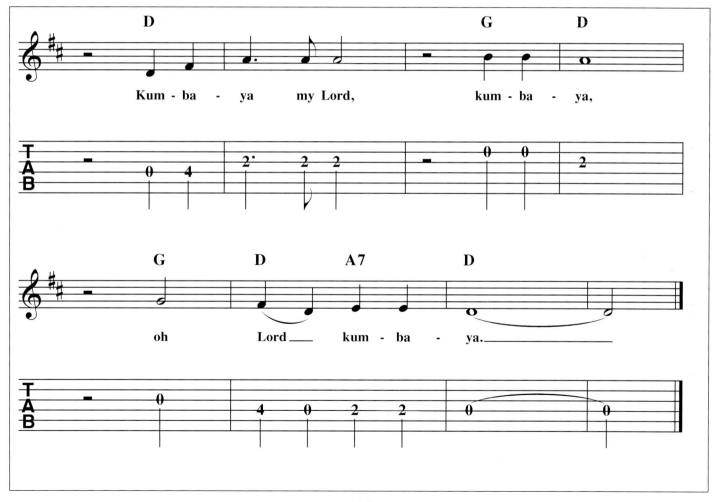

133

STRUMMING
Strumming in this tune is a matter of keeping time

We printed the melody to Kumbaya in the key of D. We also sang it in that key in the digital download. Now we'll transpose Kumbaya to the key of C so you can use the new chords. Every D chord will become a C chord, every G chord is now an F chord, and the G7 becomes an A7.

Your choice of key should mostly be governed by what key best suits your voice. Later in the book we will show you how it is also possible to change key by using a capo rather than other chord positions.

```
C               F     C
T  T  T  T   T  T T T T T   T T T T T T T
Kumbaya, my Lord, Kumbaya,
                    F   G7
T  T  T  T   T  T T T T T   T T T T T T
Kumbaya, my Lord, Kumbaya,
        C            F     C
T  T  T T   T  T T T T   T T T T T T  T T
Kumbaya, my Lord, Kumbaya,
F  C              G7     C
T T T    T       T T  T  T T T T T T
O, Lordy, won't you Kumbaya.
```

- With your right thumb, strum down across the strings. The strums are marked with a T.

```
C                        F    C
T   S   T  S    T S T ST  S  T ST ST S

Someone's singing, Lord, Kumbaya,
                         F   G7
T   S   T  S    T S T ST  S T ST ST S
Someone's singing, Lord, Kumbaya,
             C           F    C
T   S   T  S    T S T ST  T  S T ST ST S
Someone's singing, Lord, Kumbaya,
F   C              G7   C
T  S T    S      T S  T ST ST S
Oh my Lordy won't   you Kumbaya.
```

- For this arrangement strum down across the strings with two or three fingers, then strum *back* with the thumb. The rhythm is even (even eighth notes). I have marked the down strum as S, and the strum coming back as T.

YELLOW ● LIGHT

Troubleshooting:
Are you keeping good time? Can you hear all of the notes of the chord when you strum? Can you get through a whole verse without stopping to find the chord?

Be sure that you are picking evenly. Try to minimize the noise of the pick brushing across the strings. If you are getting too much pick noise, you are either exposing too much pick, or you are using a larger pick than is desirable.

```
C                  F   C
P   P  P  P    PPPP P   P  P PPPPPP
Kumbaya, my Lord, Kumbaya,
                    F   G7
P   P  P  P    PPPP P   P  P PPPPPP
Kumbaya, my Lord, Kumbaya,
      C          F   C
P   P  P  P    PPPP P   P  P PPPPPP
Kumbaya, my Lord, Kumbaya,
F  C              G7   C
P  P   P          P  P  PPPPPP
Oh Lordy, won't you Kumbaya.
```

- What you are going to play next is quite similar to the arrangement that was played by the thumb. You will now be using the flat pick, and strumming down across the strings, shown here. P means pick.

```
C                  F   C
D   U  D  U    DUDUD U  DUDUDU
Someone's shouting, Lord, Kumbaya,
                    F   G7
D   U  D  U    DUDUD U  DUDUDUDU
Someone's shouting, Lord, Kumbaya,
          C          F   C
D   U  D  U    D UDUD U  DUDUDU
Someone's shouting Lord, Kumbaya,
F  C              G7   C
DUD    U          D  U DUDUDU
Oh Lordy, won't you Kumbaya.
```

- Next try picking alternating up and down with the flat pick. You will probably play fewer strings on the way back. Be sure to play at least three or four strings, however, or the strum will be too soft. D and U mean down or uppick.

- Keep the notes even.

- No stopping for chord changes.

- Follow the dynamics of your singing.

- If you're singing loud, play loud, if you're whispering, play softly.

INTRODUCING THE WALTZ
This is our first real introduction to playing in 3/4 time

Up until now all of our songs have been written in 4/4 time, with four beats for each bar of music. 3/4 time is also known as waltz time, after a popular dance form that has three beats for each measure of music.

When you play in waltz time, you count the rhythm 1 2 3, 1 2 3, but there is an emphasis on the first beat, so that it sounds more like *1* 2 3, *1* 2 3. For now we are going to stay with the C, F, and G7 chords, and we will introduce a new piece of music, called "The Knack Waltz." First, we will go over some chord variations, and some strums that will enable you to play any song in 3/4 time. Pick up a songbook from the library, or buy one at your favorite music store. I recommend that you either look for some sort of fake book or a collection of songs that doesn't require you to have a tremendous

Full G7 Chord

- You played this one in the last chapter.

- Are you comfortable with the stretches?

- This is the standard left-hand fingering.

Full G7 Chord with Alternate LH Fingering

- This is a different left-hand fingering for the same chord.

- Which fingering you use depends on what your left hand has just played and where it will go from here.

- If you use the little finger to play the chord, you have the ring finger to play extra notes. If you use the ring finger, then the little finger is free.

vocabulary of chords. Look for a rock, country, blues, or folk songbook, because most of them don't require an extensive knowledge of chords. Be sure to choose a songbook that contains songs that you like. Why learn how to play songs that you don't want to sing or play?

C Chord with G in Bass

- Remember that I told you not to play the 6th string with the usual fingering of the C chord.

- With this left-hand fingering, you should play the 6th string.

- Many players will go back and forth between fingering the 5th and the 6th string at the 3rd fret.

- The right hand will play whichever note the left hand is fingering.

Five-string F Chord

- This is an alternate fingering of the F chord. Because you are now fingering five strings, you can now play the 5th string as one of your bass notes.

- You can also alternate playing the 5th and the 4th string, if you use this fingering.

- Remember not to play the 6th string.

3/4 STRUMS

We will now adapt some of our strums for playing in 3/4 time

One of the first strums that you learned was the one where the thumb plays bass notes and the index finger brushes down across the strings. We are now going to return to that strum, but we will modify it for waltz time. First of all, use the following sequence:

1) Thumb plays bass.
2) Index finger brushes down.
3) Index finger brushes back.

The rhythm is three even quarter notes. Try this with the C chord. Now try this variation of the strum:

Right Thumb Plays Bass

- Play the lower bass string.

- Try this with the C chord, alternately fingering the 5th and 6th string, as explained on the previous spread, and

play whichever note the left hand is fingering.

- Is your bass note clear when you move from the 6th to the 5th string?

Right Index Finger Brushes Down

- You will get a better sound with a nail than without one.

- You can also play louder with the nail.

- Remember, this is a short beat (eighth note).

1) Thumb plays bass.
2) Index finger brushes.
3) Index finger brushes back.
4) Index finger brushes down.

The rhythm is quarter note, two eighth notes, followed by another quarter note.

GREEN ● LIGHT

If you find this confusing, check out the audio track 9. That ought to help.

WALTZ TIME (3/4)

Right Index Finger Brushes Back

- Try to get at least three strings on the way back.

- This is another eighth note.

- Prepare for the next index strum.

End of Brushstroke by Index Finger

- This is a long beat (quarter note).

- If you were to continue the strum, the next note is another thumb note.

- Remember the rhythm for the entire strum is:

1 thumb
2 index down & back
3 index down

139

RIGHT-HAND VARIATION
This is another right-hand strum for 3/4 time

Stay in 3/4 time, but now we'll go back to where you learned how to use the three fingers of the right hand in the arpeggio strum. There is a certain "German beer drinking" flavor that this strum evokes.

You can alternate between using the strum with the index finger with the one that you are learning here. The more strums that you learn, the more you can vary your playing.

You can make the decision about which strum pleases you best based on your musical taste, your mood, and whether or not you are singing, or if you are playing with other musicians or singers.

Remember that in 3/4 time the emphasis is on the first beat of the measure, as in *1 2 3, 1 2 3*.

If you are using the C chord, use the fingering that alternates

Right Thumb Plays Bass

- Remember to play alternating bass notes.

- If you are playing two consecutive bass notes, like the 6th and 5th, or 5th and 4th strings, you can simply

let your thumb rest on the adjacent string before you play it.

- Notice how the addition of a bass note brings more color to your playing.

3rd, 2nd, and 1st Strings Together

- Remember that the index finger plays the 3rd string, the middle finger plays the 2nd string, and the ring finger plays the 1st string.

- Lift the fingers off the strings each time you play, in preparation for repeating this part of the strum.

between the 6th and 5th string. If you are playing the F chord with the new fingering, you can alternate between playing the 5th and 4th strings. There really isn't anything here that is new except that the rhythm is different.

3rd, 2nd, and 1st Strings Together

Right Thumb Ready to Play Higher Bass Note

WALTZ TIME (3/4)

- This is exactly the same as the last part of the strum.

- The notes should be nice and even, with a slight emphasis on the thumb beats.

- Remember to count when you play.

- This is simply where the next strum begins.

- Playing the same bass note repeatedly is boring.

- Practice the strum with all of the chords in C.

3/4 PICK PLAYING
3/4 time can just as easily be played with the use of the flat pick

The more you are able to vary between using the flat pick and the fingers, the more comfortable you will become playing in either or both styles.

Now you will be playing waltz time with the use of the pick.

You should start to think about using different sizes and materials for picks on different songs. For example, if you are playing a really soft waltz, you will want to use a small pick and to play lightly to avoid the noise of the pick brushing across the strings. If you are playing a German waltz for Oktoberfest, you will want to go to the opposite extreme and play with a pick that will provide plenty of volume. String noise isn't a problem here; in fact, if you are playing with a tuba and an accordion, or if you are only imagining these sounds in

Pick Plays 6th or 5th String

- Be sure you are able to play the note that you are looking to play, without any additional notes.

- If you don't like the sound of your pick, try a different one. Use a different shape, a different degree of thick-

ness, or try one made of another sort of material.

- Be conscious of *where* you are playing. Get accustomed to the idea of moving your hand around to get a more brittle or a more mellow attack.

Pick Brushes Down

- This should be heard as a strum, not as a single note.

- Don't play too hard.

- Be sure to keep time. You may find it easier to hear the rhythm when you use a pick.

your mind, pick noise may be downright enjoyable.

You should be beginning to feel secure enough not to be worrying about whether you may drop the pick. Your right wrist should be relaxed, and you should be able to use the pick to play for long periods of time without any strain.

Experiment with using different kinds of picks: hard, medium, or soft. You can also move your right hand toward the bridge to get a brighter sound. To get a more mellow sound, move the right hand to the top of the neck.

Pick Brushes Back

- You will have to bend your wrist to get back in position after the last strum.

- You ought to find this relatively simple.

- Practice changing the chords.

Pick Plays Higher Bass Note (4th or 5th String)

- The pick now moves over to play the 4th string if you played the 5th string for your first bass note. If you played the 6th string, you can choose between playing the 5th or 4th string.

- This is the beginning of the next strum.

"THE KNACK WALTZ"

This is the melody for "The Knack Waltz"

"The Knack Waltz" is an original melody designed to give you some practice in playing in waltz (3/4) time. Remember that these are three beats for each measure of music.

Notice that most of the notes are quearter notes. When you get to the sixth measure of the music, there are eighth notes. They can be counted as one end. In other words, each eighth note gets half a beat.

You may want to buy a songbook to look for other songs in 3/4 time.

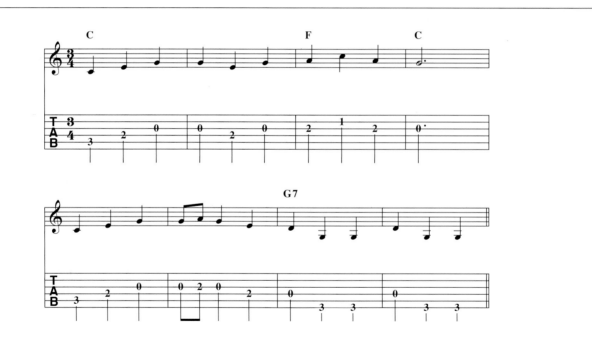

- Play through the melody with your thumb, or, if you prefer, with a pick. Don't worry about strumming.

- Be sure to play slowly, so you get the sense of the melody.

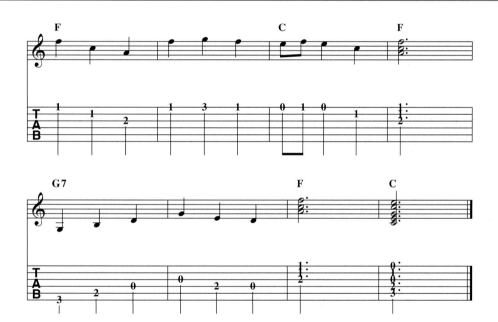

- Be sure to play slowly, and try to memorize the melody.

- Try to sing or hum the melody while using one of the 3/4 strums.

- Try a different strum while playing the second half of the melody.

"THE KNACK WALTZ," PART II
This is the same tune, with some new ways of using the right hand

The same effect can be achieved by playing the notes with a flat pick. Just as you did with your right hand fingers, be sure that each note is clear. In addition to alternating up and down picks, try to play using down picks only. This is fairly easy to do. Next try to play using up picks only. This is quite awkward at first, but is great practice.

Thumb Plays a Melody Note

- Play the entire tune with the thumb and index finger alternating, regardless of where the notes fall.

- In other words, even if there are two consecutive bass notes, alternate the thumb and index in playing the notes.

Index Plays Next Melody Note

- This style of playing is very common in the entirely unrelated technique of blues guitar playing.

146

Pick Plays Down on One Note

- Play the same tune, but with a flat pick. Alternate up and down picks.

Pick Plays Up on Next Note

- Play the chords while humming the melody notes.

- Eventually you will be able to fit melodies into strum patterns, but we're not there yet.

THE Aм CHORD

In preparation for playing some simple 1950s rock, we will now introduce the A minor chord

The A minor chord is our first minor chord. We will begin this section with it, and then, by combining it with the C, F, and G7 chords, we'll play our first rock and roll tunes.

Begin by memorizing the Am chord, which is a fairly simple task that doesn't involve much in the way of stretching the left-hand fingers.

If you go back to Chapter Eight, you will remember that the difference between a major and a minor chord is a half step, or one fret, in the third of the chord. (In the chord C E G, the E is the third of the chord.) A Cm chord contains the notes C, E♭, and G.

The Am is closely related to the C chord. In every key the

Am Chord

- There are no big secrets or special instructions here.

- The left-hand fingering is: middle finger on the 4th string at the 2nd fret, ring finger on the 3rd string 2nd fret, 1st finger on the 2nd string 1st fret.

- You can play all six strings with this chord.

- Many people describe minor chords as being "sad." I like to think of them as offering new colors.

C and Am Chord

- This is the heart of the chord progression that will enable you to play dozens of 1950s rock tunes.

- This is an easy chord change to make, because as you can see from the photo,

it only requires you to move one finger of the left hand.

- Play the two chords until they are absolutely part of your chord vocabulary.

"relative minor" of a major chord is found on the sixth note of the scale. The C scale contains the notes C D E F G A B C. You can count up from C, and see that A is the sixth note of the C scale.

This book isn't intended to be a music theory book, but every so often I attempt to add to your musical vocabulary, so you can develop some notion of the musical logic that governs your playing.

Once you can change from C to Am smoothly, you will again have extended your potential repertoire of songs.

C Going to Am

- You will need to pivot the ring finger of your left hand to make this chord change.

- Not much motion of the left wrist is required to make this shift.

Am, Coming from C

- Keep playing this chord change over and over.

- The key, as usual, is not having to look at the guitar.

Once you've achieved that level of playing ability, you're well on your way.

C, Aм, F, G7
This is the basic chord progression that screams "1950s rock"

Once you have mastered these chord changes, you are ready to rock out. There are so many songs that use this progression: "All I Have to Do Is Dream," by the Everly Brothers, "That Lucky Old Sun," "Blue Moon," "26 Miles Across the Sea," "Earth Angel," etc., etc.

We will be using the flat pick in this chapter. It is possible to play everything here with your fingers, but the pick provides a nice chunky rhythm that is entirely appropriate to the style.

If you have a collection of oldies records, or some songbooks of 1950s songs, get them out. Listen to the records and check out the songbooks. You will be amazed at how many songs use this simple chord progression, and how much fun you can have playing them.

C and Am Chords

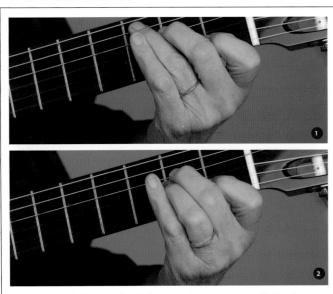

- This chord change should give you little or no trouble.

- Keep a steady beat.

- Hum to yourself. See how many songs you can think of that start with these chords.

F and G7 Chords

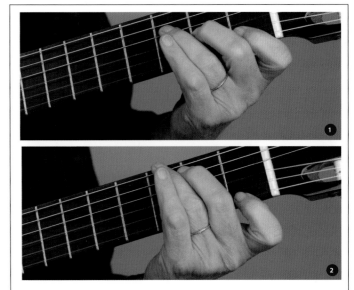

- Going from Am to F isn't as simple.

- You will need to bend the left wrist.

- Don't exaggerate the left-hand motion.

- You can use either the four- or five-string F chord.

- The F to G7 change also will require some practice.

ZOOM

Remember that the key to good guitar playing is to develop the ability to change chords with little or no hassle.

The C Am F G7 chord progression is a great building block to add even more songs to your repertoire.

Pick Style, C Chord to Am

- For the moment, don't worry about single notes, you'll be playing chords here.

- Keep your left wrist loose.

- Practice picking with different levels of intensity: loud, medium, and soft.

- Don't play the 6th string, unless you are using the alternate left-hand fingering.

Am

- You can play all six strings with this chord.

- Every string should sound cleanly.

- Keep it slow and steady.

INTRODUCING THE AM CHORD

CHORD PROGRESSION IN ACTION
Now you will start really mastering this chord progression

Rock and roll! Now that you've got the chord progression going, play it louder. Try to play it at varying tempos. The trick is for you to control the tempo, rather than having it control you. Start slowly, then speed up. See if you are able to give yourself verbal commands to play slower and faster. Are you able to do it?

You can also try playing and having someone else give you commands to play faster and slower. Once you are able to play slower or faster at will, you will have overcome your fears about changing the chords in tempo. This is another opportunity for you to record your own playing, with the verbal commands. Did you follow your own commands, or did you have to slow down the tempo to make the chord changes? Practice using dynamics—play louder, softer, moderately loud, etc.

C Chord Played with Pick

- Your wrist should now be ready to move in accordance with the necessary chord changes.

- For now, stay with down picks.

- Have you become comfortable with the flat pick?

Am Chord

- There shouldn't be any problems here.

- Try playing near the bridge, to get that nice, tinny, 1950s sound, as though you were playing a cheap electric guitar from the period.

If you can master the F chord, a whole new world of possible chords becomes available to you. The F chord can be moved up the neck to create other chords

F Chord

- If you were able to grab the F chord without hesitating, congratulate yourself!

- Make sure you are getting a good sound out of all the notes in the F chord.

- Don't get too secure, you'll be moving on to the next chord soon.

G7 Chord

- Practice playing each chord four times.

- Speed up the tempo—play faster.

- Practice changing every two beats.

UP & DOWN PICKS

You will now play the same chord progression, alternating up and down picks

It's all about controlling the use of the pick. Alternate picking up and picking down. You have already done this, but remember that every time you add a new chord to the mix, it may slow down your ability to pick. This is because you are concentrating on making the chord change.

The more time you spend on this, the easier it will become.

What takes time is developing confidence when you are up picking.

Try experimenting with the rhythm. Play up and down evenly. Try playing in 3/4 time.

Practice just doing down picks in 12/8 which is subdivided into four groups of 3, like this: 123 123 123 123. Imagine that

C Chord, Alternating Up and Down Picks

- Keep it even.

- Try making the down picked notes a little longer than the up picked notes.

Am Chord, Alternating Up and Down Picks

- This is the same pattern that you just played with the C chord.

- Did you get to the Am chord in time?

- Get ready for the more difficult change to the F chord.

you are in a doo-wop group. Your guitar is doing the equivalent of: Da da da, <u>da</u> da da, <u>da</u> da da, <u>da</u> da da. Sing along with those syllables as you're playing.

Have a friend sing this part while you are playing.

F Chord, Alternating Up and Down Picks

- Are the notes sounding good to you?

- Did you get to the F chord in rhythm?

- You should be starting to feel confident about playing this chord.

G7 Chord, Alternating Up and Down Picks

- This is the last chord in the progression.

- A chord progression is a group of chords that are connected.

- The progression will start again with the C chord.

SING A SIMPLE ROCK MELODY

You are going to sing the melody written here while you do the strum

Follow the melody written here. Follow either the music or the tablature. First play the melody on the guitar, then sing it while strumming the chords. Rock on!

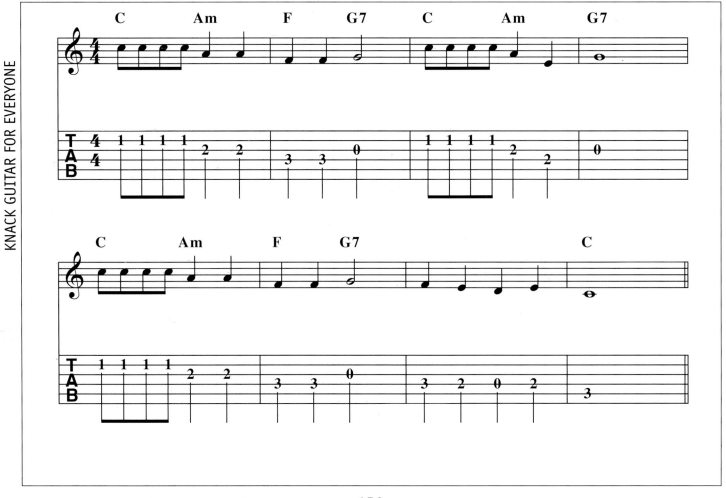

GREEN ● LIGHT

Playing this melody will give you a good start toward fig-uring out how melodies and chords go together.

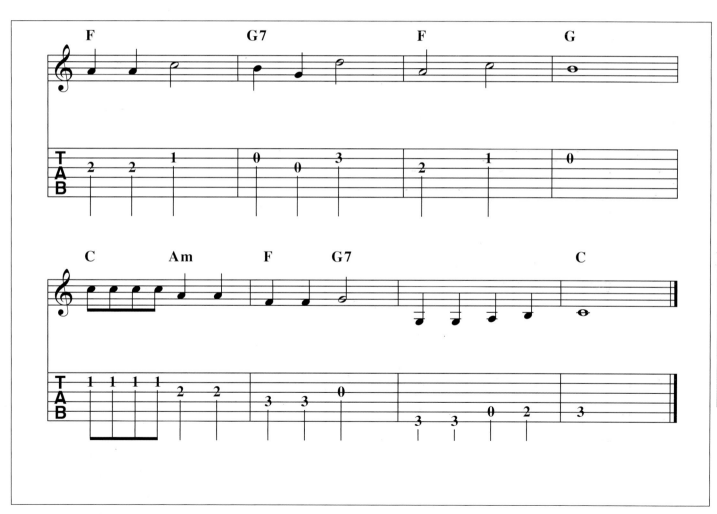

INTRODUCING THE AM CHORD

157

CREATE YOUR OWN MELODY
Try humming your own melody along with the chord progression

For the next two pages, you will be given our chord progression, and it's your job to hum a new melody! Play four beats for each chord.

Rock It!

C	Am	F	G7
C	Am	F	G7
F	G7	F	G7
C	F	C	C
Am	Am	Am	Am
F	F	F	F
G7	F	C	C

- How do you know what to sing? You don't. Experiment. If you're totally at sea, just look for melody notes in the chords you are playing.

- Think "Oh Happy Day" or "Lucky Old Sun" when you are searching for the melody.

- Be sure you don't slow down when the chords change.

Rock It!

Am	G	F	G
Am	G	F	G
C	F	C	G7
C	F	C	C
Am	F	G	F
Am	F	G	F
Am	G	Am	Am

- This chord progression has a slightly different sequence, but uses almost the same chords.

- Notice I have occasionally substituted the G for the G7.

- Again, use four beats for each chord.

Chords in 3/4 Time

C	Am	F	G7
C	Am	F	G7
C	F	C	G7
C	F	C	C
Am	Am	F	G7
Am	Am	F	G7
F	C	G7	C

- Use three beats for each chord.

- Remember you're in waltz time here. You can place a slight accent on the 1st beat.

- Now I'll throw a bunch of different rhythms at you.

- Each rhythm will be indicated by a marking at the front of the line, for example 2/4 or 4/4.

Mixing Up the Rhythm

4/4	C	Am	F	G7
	C	Am	F	G7
3/4	C	Am	F	G7
	C	F	C	C
2/4	F	G7	F	G7
	F	G7	C	C
4/4	C	Am	F	G7
	C	Am	G	G7
12/8	C	Am	F	G7
	C	F	C	C

- If you can find a melody to hum and still make the chord changes in rhythm, you're doing absolutely great.

INTRODUCING THE CAPO
The capo is a valuable and inexpensive tool for guitarists

Capos are mechanical devices that are used by guitarists to enable them to play tunes in a variety of keys without having to learn new chord positions. There are a variety of capo designs, including simple elastic capos that attach to the neck of the guitar and metal capos with spring attachments.

Let's say you are playing a song in the key of D, but the melody is a bit too low for your vocal range. You can place the capo on the 2nd fret of the guitar. You are now technically playing in the key of E, but the great news is that you can use exactly the same chords that you were playing before you placed the capo on the guitar.

Think of the guitar neck as beginning wherever the capo is placed. You will not be able to play any notes behind the fret where the capo was placed, but this is a small price to pay for

Elastic Capos

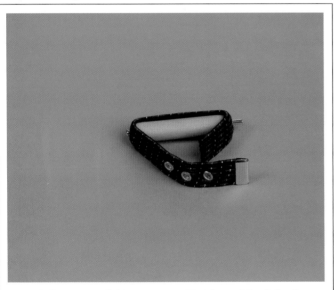

- One advantage of elastic capos is that they are inexpensive.

- Elastic capos are also very easy to place on the guitar neck.

- The downside of elastic capos is that they don't always provide enough pressure on the guitar strings to produce a good sound.

- Be careful to keep one hand on the elastic capo, because it can pop off the guitar neck and fly in your face.

Spring Capos

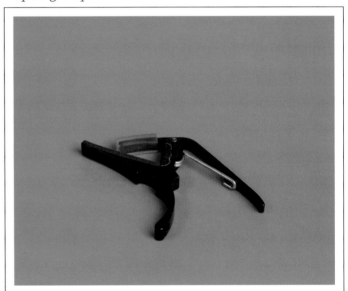

- Spring capos are readily moveable. If you are in a performing situation, this is important.

- Different manufacturers have come up with varying spring designs. Before you buy a capo, try it out to see whether it is easy to use, and produces a good sound.

- Some of the newer capos feature a design that only requires you to use one hand to place them on the guitar.

not having to learn a whole new set of chord positions. Try out different kinds of capos until you find the one that works best on your guitar.

ZOOM

There are other reasons to use the capo, which we will explain later in this chapter, that add exciting new dimensions to your guitaristic abilities.

Elastic Capo on Guitar

- Part of your choice of capo is determined by the width of the neck of your guitar.

- A very large capo doesn't work efficiently on a narrow-neck guitar. Classical guitars require a capo that will fit the width of the classical neck.

- The capo should be placed just behind the fret that you will be using.

Spring Capo on Guitar

- Be careful when you place the spring capo on the guitar. When the metal blade is open, if you are not careful, you may scratch the neck of the guitar.

- One criterion in choosing a spring capo is whether you can move the capo up and down the neck with the use of one hand.

- If you do regular performances, it's a good idea to own two capos, and to always leave one in your case.

MORE CAPOS
This section will provide some more details about capos

Placing the capo on the guitar is a reasonably simple thing to do. Keep the following guidelines in mind: Grip the capo firmly with one hand. Place the capo on the guitar on whatever fret you have chosen to place it. With the other hand connect the elastic, or the spring if you are using a spring capo. Strum across each string with the right hand to determine whether the capo is securely placed on the neck of the guitar. Each string should sound as clear as it would without the capo.

Placing Elastic Capo on Guitar

- Some of the elastic capos can be snapped together in two different places. In other words, you can adjust for the width of your neck.

- Check to make sure that the capo is on tight enough to produce a good sound.

- Make sure that the capo is straight. If it is placed crookedly, you may get some muffled strings.

Capo Now on Guitar

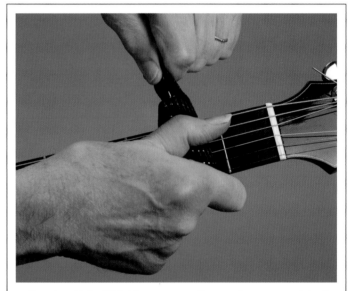

- You should find it fairly simple to place the capo on the guitar.

- Is the elastic attached securely?

- Can you hear every string?

- Practice moving the capo to different positions up and down the neck.

Placing Spring Capo

- Placing the spring capo on the guitar is simple enough to do, but a little more complicated than positioning the elastic capo.

- Be careful not to scratch the guitar neck with the capo's metal blade.

Spring Capo on Guitar

- Are the notes all clear when you strum across the strings?

- Is it comfortable for you to move the capo?

- Sometimes large capos can get in the way of your left-hand fingers.

163

VARIOUS CAPOS
These are other capo designs that are currently available

The various capo manufacturers have come up with different designs. Some metal capos have attachments that fit into the capo that must be tightened manually with your fingers. I have found that some of these capos fit quite well and are generally efficient. However, it is quite a nuisance to move them around, because you have to loosen the screw before you are able to move the capo, and then you have to tighten it when you have moved it to the position you have chosen.

This is particularly annoying to performers, who have to fill the time with audience banter while concentrating on moving the capo.

A guitar player named Harvey Reid was one of the first guitarists who experimented with using capos in a different way. Harvey's idea was to use capos that covered some of the

Various Capos Open, Not on Guitar

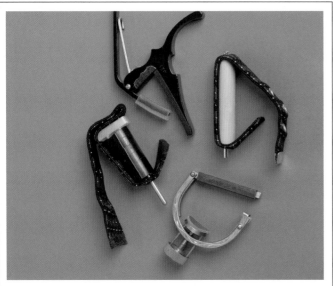

- The screw capos, as we have discussed above, are quite efficient, except for the difficulties in moving them around.

- Certain manufacturers seem to concentrate on creating different shapes of capos, contending that they apply pressure more efficiently.

- If you have a 12-string guitar, you will find that many capos don't work well on the 12-string neck, because of the pressure required to cover all of the strings.

Various Capos Closed, Not on Guitar

- You must decide for yourself which capo works best on your instrument. The choices involve the following questions:

- How moveable is the capo?

- Does it work well with your particular guitar?

- Does the guitar sound good with your capo?

strings and ignored other ones. These are known as partial capos. There are different varieties of partial capos, as you will soon see.

Partial Capo, off Guitar

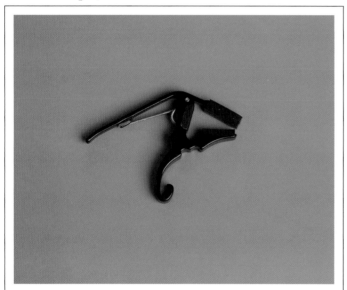

- Notice that the blade of the partial capo is smaller than the normal capo. This is because you are not covering all six strings with it.

- To use the partial capo efficiently, you have to have a good idea of what each string sounds like in different positions of the guitar neck.

This isn't as difficult as it sounds. You either have to figure out what the notes are, or work it out based upon what sounds good.

- It is also possible to use more than one partial capo, although this requires a thorough knowledge of the notes on the guitar.

Partial Capo, on Guitar

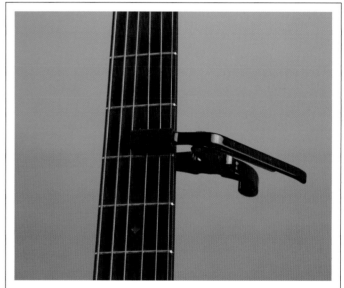

- The main issue here is: What strings do you want to sound higher in pitch?

- The relationships between the notes may sound awkward to you.

- When the capo is placed on the guitar neck, whether the capo is a normal or a

partial capo, be sure to check the tuning of your guitar. Sometimes the capo pulls some of the strings out of tune.

- Partial capos are a bit harder to find than the normal ones, but many music stores now carry them.

PARTIAL & THIRD HAND CAPOS

Besides the partial capo, there is another capo called the third hand capo

The use of partial capos has become quite involved and sophisticated, probably beyond the level where you will be dealing with them for some months. However, there is no harm in experimenting with these devices, in fact they are really fun to explore.

Randall Williams is a guitarist who has written some guitar instructional materials devoted to discussions of partial capos. I have seen Randall use as many as three capos on the guitar neck, getting an almost orchestral sound, because of the variations in the pitch of the various capoed strings.

Harvey Reid has a different method of dealing with the partial capo. Harvey created a device known as the third hand

Two Partial Capos on Guitar

- You can explore some interesting musical possibilities by placing the partial capos on different frets.

- Because the partial capo extends the range of the guitar, you can create the

sort of musical textures that an unsuspecting listener would hear as two separate instruments. (Check out audio track 23.)

Two Partial Capos at Different Frets

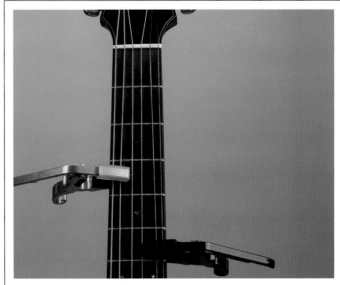

- Because of the greater fret differences, notice how the range of notes opens up.

- Try this at home (!) but don't spring it on your friends at a jam session

until you've mastered the technique.

- After a while, you will become more adept at the use of partial capos.

capo. This is an elastic capo with six rollers that you can raise and lower to mute the strings. This is a fascinating device, but operating it requires some experimentation, and even when you have figured out how you want to use it, it takes some time to move the rollers to raise and lower the strings.

Third Hand Capo, off Guitar

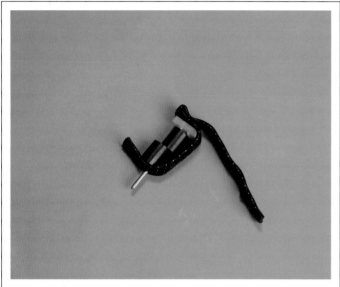

- Notice that some of the rollers are higher than others.

- As you lower the rollers, you deaden the strings.

- The effect of the third hand capo is a bit different than that of the partial capo, because you are only utilizing a single capo.

Third Hand Capo, on Guitar, Showing Muted

- As was the case with the partial capo, it takes time to develop facility in using this device.

- It can be annoying to raise and lower the rollers.

- You may have to order the third hand capo by mail, because it is not widely available in music stores.

HOW TO USE THE CAPO

Next we will explain how the capo works from a musician's point of view

You now know a bit about the various kinds of capos and how they work. The next two pages present diagrams of how the capo is used by guitarists to change keys. This involves a brief recapitulation of music theory and scales from our explorations in Chapter Eight. The notes of the musical scale in the western world are as follows:

C C# D D# E F F# G G# A A# B

Note: A C# is the same note as a D♭. An F# is the same as a G♭. Remember the symbol # means a sharped (raised) note, the symbol ♭, means flat, or a lowered note. Therefore we can also express these notes in the following way:

Without a Capo: Key of C

Capo at 1st fret	Key of C#
Capo at 2nd fret	Key of D
Capo at 3rd fret	Key of D#
Capo at 4th fret	Key of E
Capo at 5th fret	Key of F
Capo at 6th fret	Key of F#
Capo at 7th fret	Key of G

- Try different kinds of capos. Be careful to see that the guitar is still in tune.

- Once you get used to the capo, you will find that it helps you in singing songs in the key best suited for your voice.

Without a Capo: Key of D

Capo at 1st fret	Key of D#
Capo at 2nd fret	Key of E
Capo at 3rd fret	Key of F
Capo at 4th fret	Key of F#
Capo at 5th fret	Key of G
Capo at 6th fret	Key of G#
Capo at 7th fret	Key of A

- When we are playing the key of D, without a capo, this is what the capo will do:

- Capos are available at virtually any music store that sells guitars.

- If you are using a capo with a string attachment, take

care not to scatch the neck of the guitar.

- Note: Using the capo above the 7th fret is not unheard of but it isn't very efficient, because it pretty much eliminates the bass notes.

Elastic Capo

- The reason you need to check your tuning when you use the capo is because it sometimes pulls the strings, which causes them to go out of tune.

Spring Capo

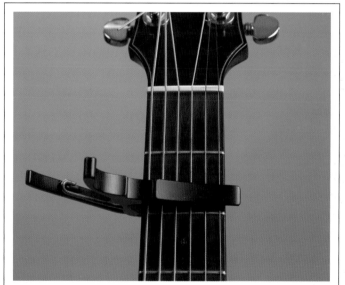

- Be sure the capo is firmly closed or it can spring off the guitar. If you're using any sort of capo that contains metal, this can injure you or someone else.

TWO GUITARS & THE CAPO

When playing with another guitarist, often one player uses the capo, and the other one does not

Another use of the capo occurs when two guitarists get together to jam. One guitarist may play without the use of the capo, while the other one uses the capo. For example, if you look back at the capo diagrams, the key of D can be played by playing D chords without the use of the capo, but it can also be played if you place the capo on the neck at the 2nd fret and play in the key of C.

Let's say that the chords of the song that you decide to play are C, F, and G7 in the key of C.

The guitarist using the capo at the 5th fret can play the chords G, C, and D7, and the two guitarists will be playing in the same key. There are a number of reasons for doing this.

Guitarist without Capo

Chords of the song in the key of C:
4/4 time

C///   C///   F///   F///

C///   C///   G7//   C

- Now I will recapitulate the diagrams of what the capo does, but in a different way.

- Let's imagine that you are playing in the key of C, but you want to hear another guitar playing a part in a higher pitch, and your jamming partner isn't an experienced player who can find a part high up the neck.

- Some of what I am going to ask your friend to do goes slightly beyond your chord knowledge, but by referring to the diagrams, you should be able to follow this explanation.

Guitarist with Capo at 5th Fret, Key of G

4/4 time

G///   G///   C///   C///

G///   G///   D7///   G///

- Have your friend place her capo on the 7th fret of the guitar. She will play chords that are actually in the key of G, but because of the capo, they will actually be in the same key as you are. Follow the diagram above.

- Remember: Each chord name and slash (/) receives one strum. For now either strum with your right thumb or with a pick.

Because of the chord formations, the two guitarists will be playing different open strings (the ones that are not fingered in the left hand).

A good example of the above point is that a C chord has an open 1st string, but a D chord does not.

ZOOM

Troubleshooting: If you do not make the chord changes together, this will sound terrible! Notice that even though you are both doing essentially the same thing, somehow it sounds different and interesting. This is because you play in different registers of the guitar, and because each chord has its own particular sequence of intervals.

Guitar Playing in D, No Capo

3/4 time

D//   D//   A7//   A7//

D//   D//   G//   G//

D//   D//   A7//   A7//

G//   G//   D//   D

- Here is one more example that is designed to help you understand how the capo works.

- This time one guitar will be playing in the key of D, without a capo, and the other will be playing with a capo on the 2nd fret in the key of C. Follow the diagrams above.

Guitar with Capo at 2nd Fret, Chords in C

3/4 time

C//   C//   G7//   G7//

C//   C//   F//   F//

C//   C//   G7//   G7//

F//   F//   C//   C

- Remember: Three beats for each bar of music. Only one beat on the last chord, because the tune ends here.

INTRODUCING THE CAPO

ANOTHER SET OF CHORDS

Here is another set of chords and an arrangement that uses the capo

This section not only introduces the key of G, but also your second minor chord. (If you are thinking, "minor chord, what's a minor chord?", saunter back to Chapter Eight.)

The keys of C and D are fairly close together, musically, but the key of G is quite a bit higher in musical pitch. (Remember the scale, C D E F G A B C?) Look at how close together C and

D are, and how distant they both are from the key of G.

The other purpose of this chapter is to give you some actual examples of how the capo is utilized on the guitar. Since you have already learned the G and C chords, the new chords on this block are D7 and Em. Neither of them require much in the way of left-hand stretches.

G Chord

- This is the same old G chord you used in the key of D. No surprises here, still the same mildly annoying stretch.

- The biggest challenge in playing the G chord is moving from it to other chords, or in moving back to the G from other chords.

C Chord

- Again, this one is a replay, and shouldn't cause you any particular problems.

- Are you happy with the sound that you get when you play the chord?

- Be sure you have cut the nails of your left hand short.

- Remember not to play the 6th string.

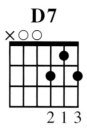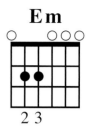
Practice changing from G to C to D7 to G to Em, until you feel comfortable making the chord changes. As you build up your chord vocabulary, you will be able to play more and more songs, and you will also be able to accompany your singing in more appropriate keys.

D 7

E m

2 1 3

2 3

D7 Chord

- Another fairly simple chord. The left hand fingering is:

- 2nd finger at the 3rd string 2nd fret, 1st finger on the 2nd string at the 1st fret, and 3rd finger on the 1st string at the 2nd fret.

- Don't play the 6th string.

- Moving from D7 back to G requires a fair amount of wrist mobility.

Em Chord

- You can play all six strings with this chord.

- This may be the easiest chord you will ever play on the guitar! Consider it a reward!

- The 2nd finger of the left hand plays the 5th string at the 2nd fret, and the 3rd

finger plays the 4th string at the 2nd fret.

- Practice changing from G to Em. If you remember playing C to Am, the relationships between the two pairs of chords are similar (major chord to relative minor).

PRACTICAL CAPO USE

"Tell Old Bill" will be written in G, but I want you to place your capo on the 1st fret

The purpose of this section is to show you the practicalities of using the capo. The chords that you will be using for "Tell Old Bill" are the ones shown in the photos, G, Em, C, and D7. With the capo on the 1st fret, you will actually be playing A♭, Fm, D♭, and E♭7 (remember I could have named these chords as G#, Fm, C#, and D#7).

As I previously explained, G# and A♭ are the same notes, as are D♭ and C#, as well as E♭ and D#.

The only reason for mentioning all of this is that if you are jamming with a piano player, they will be playing in the key of A♭, not G. Piano players don't use capos (except for the song-writer Irving Berlin, who actually did have the equivalent of

G Chord with Capo at 1st Fret

- Remember, this is, musically speaking, actually an A♭ or G# chord.

- Guitarists who have really large hands may find that the capo gets in the way of playing chords with the left hand. For now it may seem a bit awkward, but you ought to be able to get used to it quickly.

- Sometimes the left hand can hit the capo and actually move it.

Em Chord with Capo at 1st Fret

- When you use the capo, remember the guitar now begins where the capo is placed.

- This is an easy chord without the capo and an easy chord with it.

- If only every chord were this easy.

- Musically speaking, this is actually an Fm chord.

a capo on his piano, an odd crank mechanism that enabled him to always play with the same fingerings while he altered the key with the crank).

C Chord with Capo at 1st Fret

- This is actually a D♭ chord.

- It may feel to you as though the capo is in the way of your left hand.

- Practice changing the chords with the capo in place.

D7 Chord with Capo at 1st Fret

- This is actually an E♭ 7 chord.

- You still need to avoid playing the 6th string with this chord.

- Practice changing back and forth from G to D7 (A♭ to E♭ 7)

CAPO AT THE 2ND FRET

This is exactly what you have just done, but with the capo placed at the 2nd fret

It is critically important for you to get used to playing in different capo positions. When you place the capo at the 2nd fret, the key of G actually becomes the key of A. The chords G, Em, C, and D7 are now actually A, F#m, D, and E7.

You will notice that as you place the capo farther up the neck, the distance between the frets becomes smaller. The stretches will become smaller, which is great if you have small hands, good if you have medium-size hands, and may prove quite annoying if you have large hands.

There is absolutely nothing new in this section, except that the capo is at the 2nd fret. You shouldn't experience any difficulties to speak of in playing "Tell Old Bill" at the 2nd fret. At

G Chord, Capo at 2nd Fret

- Exactly what you did two pages ago, but with the capo moved up one fret.

- When you change chords, once you get used to the chord, you should be changing with your whole

left hand. In other words, you shouldn't move the chord one finger at a time, or you will never be able to play in an accurate rhythm.

- This is now actually an A chord.

Em Chord, Capo at 2nd Fret

- This is now actually an F# minor chord.

- Still as easy to play as it was before.

- All six strings should be strummed.

least you shouldn't experience any *new* problems here.

Experiment with playing the chord sequence in a different order, like Em to G to D7 to C, or in any order that amuses you. As usual, the idea is to become so accustomed to the chord changes that they feel like second nature to you.

C Chord, Capo at 2nd Fret

- If you're feeling adventurous, practice alternating the bass note between the 5th string at the 3rd fret, and the 6th string at the 3rd fret. To do this, you will need to

take the finger that was on the 5th string and move it over to the 6th string.

- This is actually a D chord now.

D7 Chord, Capo at 2nd Fret

- This is actually an E7 chord now.

- Don't play the 6th string.

"TELL OLD BILL"

This is the melody of the old vaudeville-flavored song, "Tell Old Bill"

This is the melody to "Tell Old Bill" in music and tab. Notice that the chord progression is very much like what we played for a 1950s rock song, but because the order of the chords is different, it doesn't sound at all like a 1950s rock tune.

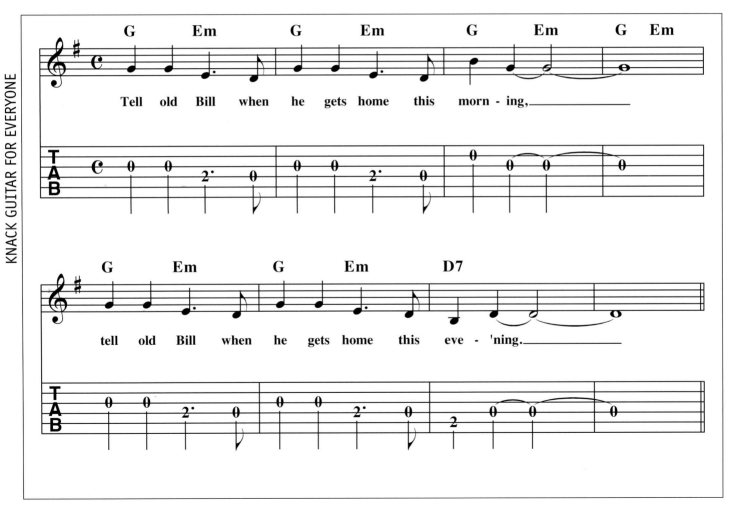

ZOOM

Sing along with this song: Bill's wife she was baking bread this morning / Bill's wife she was baking bread this evening / Bill's wife she was baking bread when she got news her man was dead / This morning, this evening so soon.

Oh no it can't be so this morning / Oh no it can't be so this evening / Oh no it can't be so, he left home just an hour ago / This morning, this evening so soon.

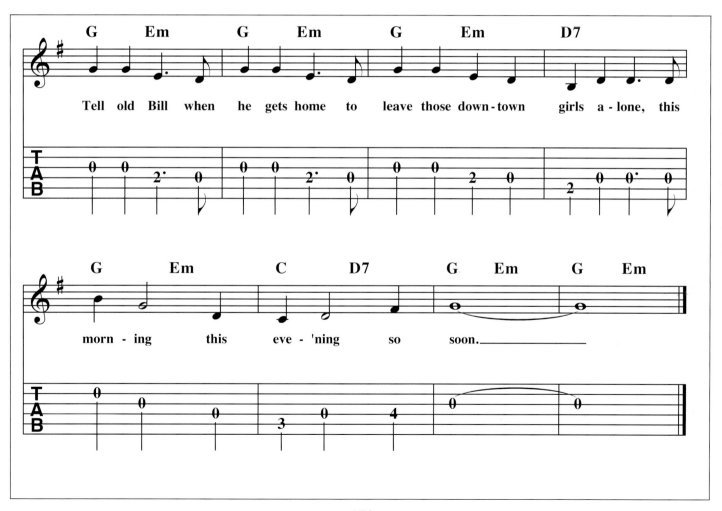

STRUM FOR "TELL OLD BILL"

We'll start with the arpeggio, and then expand upon it

Initially you will use the guitar arpeggio for this song. We will introduce a variation to show you how you can enrich your playing by changing the strum in the context of an individual song.

To capture the flavor of this tune, you need to pause very slightly after each thumb note. This will give a sort of laid-back and casual feel to the tune. The way that you should

utilize the strum with the song is shown below:

The pattern is:

1) Thumb plays bass.
2) Index plays 3rd string.
3) Middle finger plays 2nd string.
4) Ring finger plays 1st string.

Right Thumb on Bass

- Remember, the thumb note is slightly longer than the other notes.

- Vary the bass notes, as we did earlier—low bass, high bass.

- It will help you to grasp the rhythm if you let the thumb come to rest on the next string below it after each strum.

1st Finger of RH Picks Up 3rd String

- The note should be precise.

- Keep the right hand arched.

- After you play the string, come off it.

I have deliberately only given you the first line of the strum. If you have trouble, play along with audio track 27.

T I MR TIM R TI M R TIM R TI MR
Tell old Bill, when he gets home, this morning
(play TIMR four times before going on)

Tell old Bill, when he gets home this evening,

Tell old Bill, when he gets home, to leave those downtown girls alone,

This morning, this evening so soon.

2nd Finger of RH Picks Up on 2nd String

- One finger to a string!

- Sing the melody, or hum it.

- Try practicing this with audio track 27.

Ring Finger of RH Picks Up on 1st String

- The sequence is then repeated.

- The sound should be smooth and casual.

- Your thumb should be ready to play again.

A NEW STRUM

This strum combines the arpeggio with the thumb-index strum

By combining strums you can greatly enrich your playing. You will enjoy it more, and so will anyone who is listening to you. Here are the necessary steps:

1) Thumb plays high bass string.
2) Index plays 3rd, middle plays 2nd, ring plays 2nd (together).

3) Thumb plays low bass string.
4) Index brushes down across strings.

The rhythm can be even, or you can take the slightest of pauses after the first thumb note.

For just the first part of line one:

Right Thumb Plays Bass String

- Nothing new here.

- Remember to play the lower bass note.

- The three fingers should be in position ready to play.

Three Fingers Play 3rd, 2nd, and 1st Strings

- One finger to a string.

- Pluck the strings up, toward you.

- Ready for the next thumb note.

T I MR TIM R TI M R TI M R   TI MR
Tell old Bill, when he gets home this morning

Don't forget that the index, middle, and ring fingers are playing together.

Right Thumb Plays Bass

- Remember, if you played the 6th string with the last thumb stroke, you can play the 5th or 4th string now. If you played the 5th string first, play the 4th string now.

- Ready to brush down with the index.

Index Finger of RH Brushes Down

- Like one of your earliest strums.

- Brush across at least the highest three strings.

- Practice this strum without the song too.

HAMMERING ON

Hammering on is a technique where the left hand plays notes on its own

In this chapter you will be introduced to the left-hand technique called "hammering on."

Hammering on is a technique that involves the use of the left hand to play notes. Normally it is the right hand that plays notes, but with hammering on the left hand can assume that role as well.

With your left hand, finger the 1st string at the 2nd fret. Now take your finger off the fret. Play the 1st string open. Quickly, but not hurriedly, play the 1st string at the 2nd fret with your left hand. You will then hear another note. (The two notes are the open E string, and the F♯, which you have hammered on.)

Hammering On on 4th String, Open

- Are the notes clear?

- Can you hear both notes equally strong?

- Are you pressing too hard, or not hard enough?

Hammering On at 4th String, 2nd Fret

- Are the two notes clearly audible?

- The motion of the hammering needs to be done without hesitation.

- This technique is extremely useful.

It's as simple as that. It is also possible to hammer on an entire chord. For example, finger the A7 chord. Take your left-hand fingers off the chord. Strum across the top four open strings, and then play the chord with the left hand.

To get a good sound when you hammer on, you cannot play the left-hand notes too soon, or you will not hear the initial notes clearly. On the other hand, if you wait too long before you do the hammers, the hammered-on notes won't sound clearly.

It takes a bit of practice, but it's not really that difficult. . . .

You need to experiment with the technique to find out how hard you need to play with the left hand. Your goal should be to make the notes as clear as the ones you pick with the right hand.

Hammer at 3rd String, 2nd Fret

- The other fingers need to stay on the chord.

- If you're confused about the correct sound, listen to audio track 28.

- The right hand can play the first note with the thumb, index finger, or a flat pick.

2nd String, Hammer at 2nd String, 3rd Fret

- Try not to move the other fingers.

- In a while we will integrate hammers with strums.

- It should be getting easier by now.

HAMMERING ON CHORDS

It is possible to use hammering on with entire chords, as well as notes

Hammering on an entire chord sounds particularly good with strums. It is accomplished in the same way as what you have just played, except it is now the entire chord that is being hammered.

Finger an A7 chord with the left hand. Now take your left-hand fingers off the chord. Strum across the strings with either a flat pick or your thumb or index finger. Next finger the chord with the left hand.

The sound, which you can hear on audio track 28, is almost like the sound of a train. Try playing the hammers four times on the A7 chord. What you are striving for here is more of a rhythmic attack than playing individual strings. Be careful to

Ready to Hammer On the D Chord

- It is critical that your left hand lands on the proper chord notes. Prepare your left hand to play the chord.

- If you can possibly record your playing, do so. Listen back critically.

- Play along with the audio track.

Hammer On Entire D Chord

- Do both chords sound good to you?

- Don't play the 6th string.

- You can play the 5th and 4th strings.

186

come down on the chord notes precisely. If you miss a string, you're going to play the wrong note.

Hammering on is an extremely common device in country and folk music.

Preparing to Hammer On Entire A7 Chord

- Are you ready to finger the chord?

- You can play all six strings with this chord.

- Don't rush.

Hammer On A7 Chord

- You should be now reaching the point where your fingers are well prepared for the hammers.

- Are you getting a good sound?

- Practice playing the open D, hammering on the D, playing the open A7, and hammering on the A7.

HAMMERING THE G CHORD

The G chord involves a longer stretch in the left hand; try it with hammering on

Hammering on the G chord is quite effective, because you have two bass notes to choose from. Bass notes sound great hammering on.

You may find hammering on with G a bit tougher, because of the long left-hand finger stretch that is required to finger the chord. Don't go too fast, and you should be able to handle it after some practice sessions. Remember, if you are hammering on single notes in the chord, you should be able to hear the open string and the hammered note equally clearly.

G Chord, 6th String Open Prior to Hammering

- The 6th string is the one that requires the most pressure to execute hammers.
- Don't press *too hard* with the left-hand finger.
- Keep your left wrist relaxed.

G Chord, Hammer On at the 6th string, 3rd fret

- Be careful not to hammer from too high above the fingerboard.
- Practice slow, then faster, then slow, etc.
- If your bass string is wearing out, change it.

MAKE IT EASY

If you can't hear the first note, then your left hand has moved too quickly. If you can't hear the hammered note, then you either waited too long to do the hammer or your left hand isn't playing strongly enough. Remember that hammering on is a bit unnatural, because up until now you have only used the left hand to play chords or to finger individual melody notes that the right hand was picking.

G Chord, 5th String Open Ready to Hammer

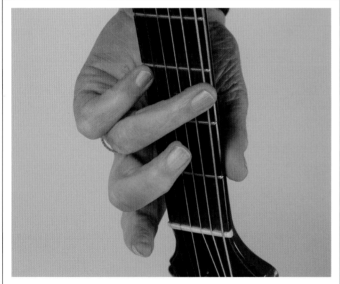

- It is very easy for the left hand to slide off the 6th string while you are playing the open 5th string. Don't let this happen.

- Are you hearing any buzzing from other strings? If so, you are not playing the 5th string cleanly.

- You should prepare the left-hand finger for the hammered note.

G Chord, Hammer On 5th String, 2nd Fret

- Both notes should be clear, and equally audible.

- Be sure the other left-hand fingers remain on the chord.

- Practice the G hammer-ons consecutively, 6th string open, 6th string hammered at the 3rd fret, 5th string open, 5th string hammered at the 2nd fret.

A MINOR HAMMERS

Am is a particularly good chord for hammering on.

The reason that Am works so well with this technique is that the chord is laid out so that the three strings that are fingered are all adjacent to one another. There are no stretches, and it's an easy chord to play, so it's the perfect vehicle for the hammering-on technique.

We're going to hammer on all of the chord notes separately, beginning with the 4th string.

By now you should have a pretty good idea of how hard you will need to press on the strings with the left hand, and your wrist should have developed the muscle memory to do the technique with minimal difficulty.

I assume that you can play the Am chord without difficulty, and that you have a good enough grasp of hammering on to be able to hear the sound that you are striving to play.

Am Chord, 4th String Open, Prior to Hammer

Am Chord, Hammer on 4th String, 2nd Fret

- Because the strings are adjacent, you may find the left-hand fingers brushing into each other. Try to prevent this from occurring.

- If your open string doesn't sound clear, there is no way that you can execute the hammer in a musical way. What you will have is *two* unclear notes.

- Try to minimize any motion by the other left-hand fingers.

- Both notes should be equally strong.

- Don't let the other left-hand fingers move while you hit the hammered note.

- Practice your hammers for ten to fifteen minutes every day when you pick up the guitar.

YELLOW ● LIGHT

If hammering on is proving difficult for you, ask a more experienced guitarist to try it on your guitar. Are the strings reasonably fresh? Is the neck in good enough condition that you can play without too much effort?

Am Chord, 3rd String Open, Prior to Hammer

- Because the left-hand finger is the ring finger, you may find this a bit more awkward than the previous hammer.

- It is a good idea to practice the things you have trouble playing when you first pick up the guitar. If you stay with this method, you should see gradual improvement, or even rapid advancement, in your technical abilities.

- Beware of not practicing things that you have mastered, simply because they sound good to you. This won't help you to progress.

Am Chord, Hammer On at 3rd String, 2nd Fret

- This may be more difficult for you than the previous hammer, which was played by the middle finger.

- Don't let the other left-hand fingers move.

- Try not to brush the other left-hand fingers as you do the hammered note.

191

MORE A MINOR HAMMERS
This will complete the hammering-on technique for the A minor chord

You should be able to hammer on all of the Am notes without too much difficulty. In this section we will finish the first exercise and "fill in the blanks," adding additional A minor hammers.

Practice alternating the various hammers that you have tried with the Am chord. Start slowly, and pick up the pace as

you find yourself able to:

- Get a good sound
- Play in time
- Avoid hitting extraneous notes

The ultimate test is when someone cannot tell the difference

Am Chord, 2nd String Open, Before Hammer

- This is quite a bit easier than hammering on the 3rd string, because no other left-hand fingers are in the way.

- Still, beware of other left-hand fingers intruding or leaving the fingerboard.

- You may want to use the right index finger to pick this note. Generally speaking, the right thumb avoids playing on the higher strings.

Am Chord, Hammer On 2nd String, 1st Fret

- You can practice the left-hand fingers hammering on the chord notes individually.

- In other words, 4th string open, 4th string hammer, 3rd string open, 3rd string hammer, 2nd string open, 2nd string hammer, and back.

- This exercise will also help you develop more strength in the left hand.

- It will also increase the flexibility of each left-hand finger.

192

between the notes that you are playing with the right hand and the ones that you are playing with the left hand.

When you hear both notes played back on a recording device, can you hear the difference? If you can, you need to practice more slowly, until you can clearly articulate each note or chord, open or hammered.

With sufficient practice, and a minimally decent guitar, you ought to be able to accomplish these goals.

Open Strings, Ready to Play Am Chord

- Once again you are going to hammer on an entire chord.

- All the left-hand fingers should be poised to make the chord.

- You shouldn't find this too difficult.

Hammer on Entire Am Chord

- All of the left-hand fingers are now on the chord.

- As usual, we are looking for clarity, correct left-hand fingering, and clean articulation of all of the notes.

- The next step will be to try a musical exercise with hammered on notes.

HAMMERED MELODY

This is a melody that requires virtually continuous hammering on

"Harry's Hammer" is a melody that requires you to use hammering on all notes. You can hear it on audio track 30.

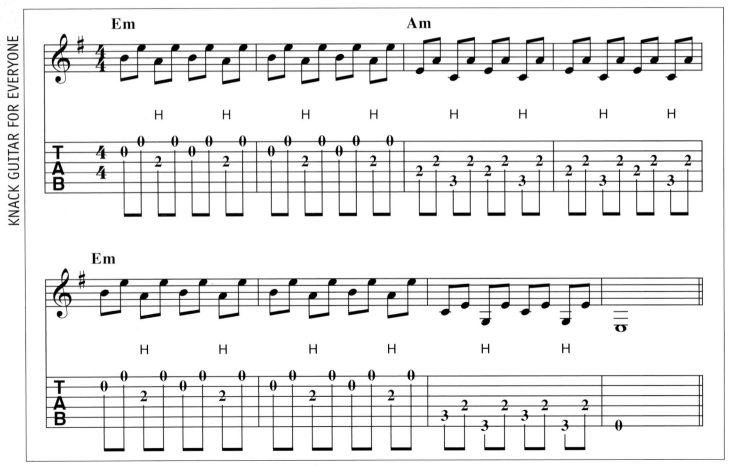

194

Hammered notes sound best when they are articulated so clearly that the listener connot tell the difference between notes played by the left and right hands.

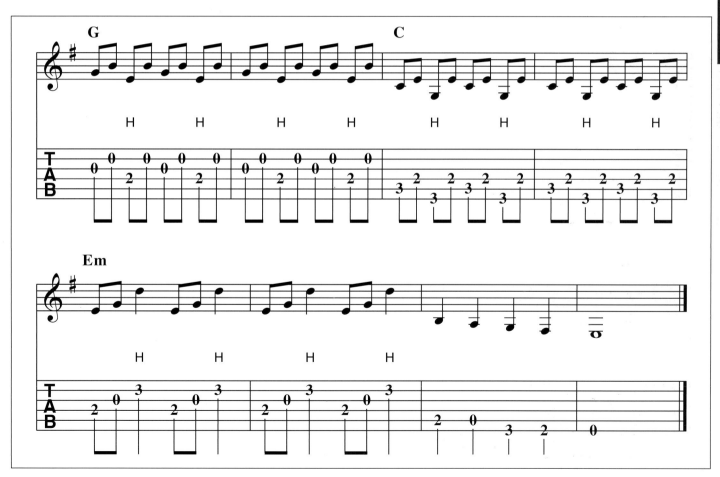

HAMMERING NON-CHORD NOTES

It is also possible to hammer on notes that aren't in a chord

Now that you have gotten used to hammering on notes that are in the chord, let's take a look at some other hammering-on possibilities. We'll start with our old friend the D chord. The notes that you will be hammering on are on the 4th and 5th strings. These notes aren't in the D chord, and you haven't fingered them before.

You are probably wondering how you can tell which notes you can hammer on. Obviously some notes that aren't in the chord sound bad when you play the other notes that are in the chord. Usually the hammered notes that aren't in the chords will be what we refer to as neighbor notes. Neighbor notes are notes adjacent to the chord. Often they can be played when you return quickly to the notes that are in the chord.

D Chord, Showing Open 4th

- Your first finger is going to be moving off the 3rd string to the 4th string, so be ready to make that move.

- Keep the left hand arched, and relaxed.

- Remember, the note you just played and the one you are going to play are of equal value.

D Chord, Hammer 4th String, 2nd Fret

- Remove your left-hand index finger from 3rd string.

- You will leave the 4th string, where the index finger was, as an open string.

- You may have to push a little harder than you generally have done with hammered notes.

- This technique opens up a whole new music vocabulary.

I call this technique "advanced hammering on," because of the fact that the notes that you will be playing here are not in the chord.

••••••••••••••••• RED●LIGHT ••••••••••••••
You will need to have good control over your hammers to pull this technique off.

ADVANCED HAMMERING ON

D Chord, 5th String Open

- We are going to do the same thing that you just did, this time on the 5th string.

- Don't rush!

- This is a bit longer for your index finger to travel, so be ready.

D Chord, Hammer 5th String, 2nd Fret

- Once you get this under control, you can alternate the hammer on the 4th and 5th string with the D chord fingered in the left hand.

- Throw in an occasional strum just to see what the chord sounds like with a note that you used to finger in the left hand now

an open string. It uses a note that you didn't play in the previous D chord fingerings.

- Check what this sounds like on audio track 30.

A7 HAMMERS

Now we'll see how this works with the A7 chord

The next step is to try a similar series of hammers with the A7 chord. With the hammers given here, it is particularly enjoyable to alternate the bass notes, as you will soon see, on the 5th and 4th strings.

First we're going to play the note on the 4th string that you have already learned, the 4th string at the 2nd fret. The A7 chord is one of the easiest chords to play, so this shouldn't prove too difficult. Pick bass notes with your right thumb, or with a flat pick. If you choose to use the flat pick, don't play too loud, because it will be difficult for you to match the volume with the left-hand hammers.

- Don't let your left wrist "slump."
- Move your left hand quickly, without any jerky motions.
- Listen carefully to the sound you are getting.

A7 Chord, with LH Not Fingering 4th String

- Lift the middle finger of the left hand off the string.
- Did the first note sound clear to you?

- Be ready to come down on the 4th string at the 2nd fret with the middle finger.

A7 Chord, Hammer On 4th String, 2nd Fret

- This is old news and shouldn't give you any problems.
- Next we'll try the advanced version.

- If it doesn't sound good, there's a reason for it. Try to figure it out for yourself.

A7 Chord, 5th String Open

- You are going to move your left middle finger off the 4th string to the 5th string, so be ready to do that.

- If you have a large-bodied guitar, don't pick the string too hard or the sound will be "boomy."

Hammer 5th String, 2nd Fret

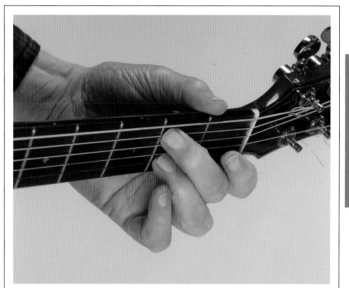

- This is the alternating bass pattern, moving from the 4th to the 5th string.

- Remember, you are playing this note with the left hand alone, so your fingering needs to be quick and decisive.

- For fun, try the same thing with the 6th string at the 2nd fret.

E MINOR HAMMERS
We'll now try advanced hammering on with the E minor chord

The Em chord sounds great with hammering on because it is an easy chord to play, and the bass note of the chord is a low E, which sounds rich and powerful. We will start off by hammering on the whole chord, then hammer on some of the notes in the chord, before moving on to notes that are not in the normal Em fingering.

The Em chord only requires two fingers of the left hand, so it is a simple chord to play. If you take a look at the Em chord, you will see that the highest three strings of the guitar don't use any fingers of the left hand. By now you should have figured out that this will leave plenty of notes for you to hammer. For now let's stick to the chord, and work up from there. Keep your left wrist arched in preparation for the hammered notes.

LH Fingers Right above Em Chord Ready to:

- Because this is such a simple chord, you should be able to get a good hammering-on sound without a great deal of effort.

- Sometimes if the notes don't sound good to you, it's because the guitar is out of tune.

- Check your tuning.

- Get ready to finger the notes of the Em chord with the left hand.

Hammer On Entire Em Chord

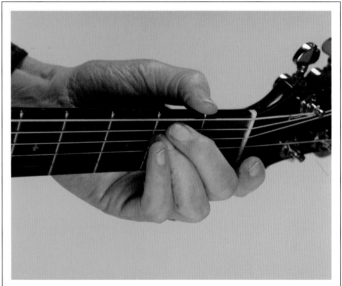

- As with the A minor chord, there is something about hammering on this chord that has a train sound to it. Try hammering on the chord, and then strumming, and that accentuates that sound.

- When you hammer on, don't pull the strings, just place your fingers on them. If you pull the strings, you may put the guitar out of tune.

MAKE IT EASY

You should be able to get a great sound out of the Em chord. If the notes don't sound good to you, you should definitely have a friend or a guitar teacher check out your guitar and also watch you play.

ADVANCED HAMMERING ON

Em Chord, 5th String Open

- You are now about to hammer the note on the 5th string at the 2nd fret.

- Be sure that you are ready to get the left-hand middle finger on the 5th string without any delay.

- This should sound really good to you!

Em Chord, Hammer On at 5th String, 2nd Fret

- The hammered note should be rich and full.

- Listen to this on audio track 31.

- Hammering on is great fun, and by now you should be enjoying it!

MORE E MINOR HAMMERS
We will now apply hammers on Em to notes that are not in the chord

Just as we tried advanced hammers with the previous chords, you can now add extra notes to the Em that are not part of the actual chord. The notes we'll add are on the 3rd and 6th strings.

The note on the 3rd string is an A, which is not in the Em chord, but it is a neighbor note, in fact kind of a double

neighbor, because it lies between the G and B notes, both of which are indeed part of the E minor chord. The note on the 5th string is a G, and this is actually in the Em chord, but this fingering is not usually used, because the open 6th string is an E, and it is a stronger note in the chord. However, we will be going back and forth between the G and the E, so you

Em Chord, 4th String Open

- This chord actually sounds pretty good with the open 5th string because it is an E, which is a suspended 4th in an E chord.

- Ring finger should prepare to play the note on the 3rd string 2nd fret.

- Hammered notes must be accurate, or the sound is muddy.

Em Chord, Hammer On at 3rd String, 2nd Fret

- This extra note is called a suspended 4th, and you almost always play the G note (3rd string open) immediately after you play the A.

- Don't remove your left-hand middle finger from the 5th string.

- Practice playing the note on the 4th string 2nd fret open, the 2nd string 2nd fret, and then doing exactly the same thing on the 3rd string.

should find that sound to be pleasing.

The more notes you can add to your playing that lie outside the chord notes, the more interesting your playing will become. Obviously anyone can learn to play chords out of a chord book.

YELLOW ● LIGHT

When you play the open note on the 6th string, be careful not to hit it too hard, or the sound will be overly bass-heavy.

Em Chord with 6th String Open

- Play the 4th string, with the left hand fingering the note at the 4th string 2nd fret.

- Prepare the little finger of the left hand to play the note on the 6th string at the 3rd fret.

- Fingering notes with the little finger is a bit harder than using any of the other left-hand fingers, because the little finger tends to be weaker and less agile.

Em Chord, Hammer On 6th String, 3rd Fret

- You can alternate playing the 6th string note at the 3rd fret with playing the 6th string open.

- Be sure to press firmly with the little finger.

- Practice all of the various Em hammers.

HAMMERING PLUS

Hammering plus is an exercise that will give you practice in advanced hammering on

This exercise consists entirely of advanced hammering until
the last two bars of music. Play this one with your thumb and
index finger, with or without picks, or with a flat pick.

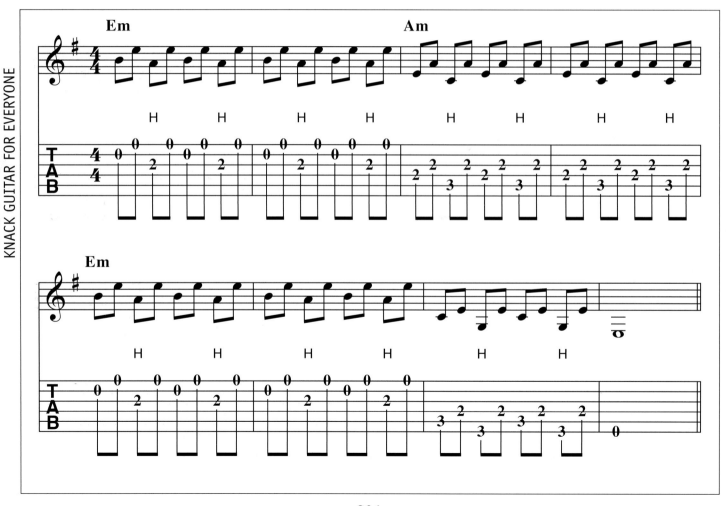

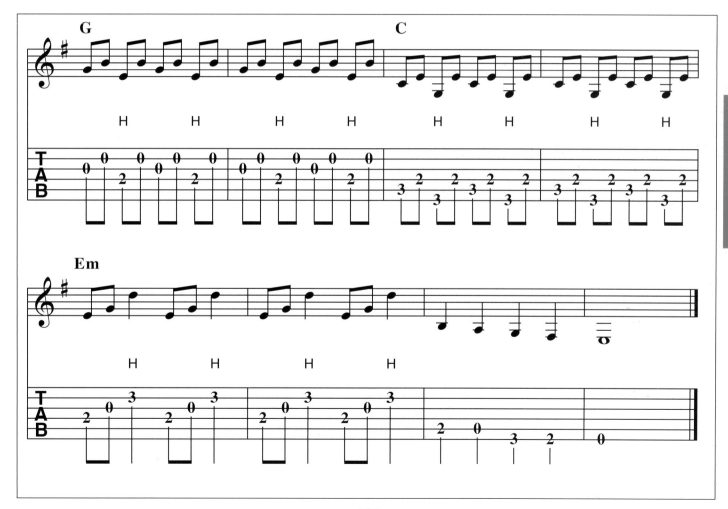
ZOOM

It takes time to get the hang of hammering on.
Be patient, and try to record some of your playing.
Listen to see if you are getting a good sound.

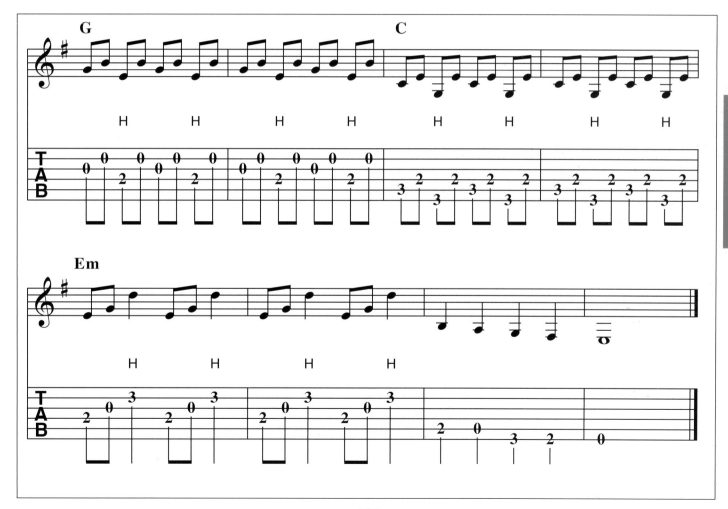

ADVANCED HAMMERING ON

RIGHT-HAND POSITION

This chapter introduces fingerpicking, also known as Travis picking

Fingerpicking is an exciting guitar style. It is a style that has been used by blues and country music virtuoso guitarists. It is a loose combination of ragtime and nineteenth-century parlor guitar styles. Country music stars Merle Travis and Chet Atkins, and blues guitarists Mississippi John Hurt and Furry Lewis all used variations of it. You can hear this technique today on many country and folk recordings done by such artists as Peter, Paul & Mary, Jerry Reed, Joan Baez, Leo Kottke, and many others.

Fingerpicking can be done with just the thumb and index fingers, but it is probably more common to use the thumb, index, and middle fingers of the right hand. Some players also toss in the ring finger.

The first part of this chapter is devoted to the right-hand

RH Ring Finger Resting near Sound Hole

- The most common right-hand position for finger-picking has the ring finger resting on the guitar near the sound hole. This provides support for the other fingers.

- The weakness of this position is that it prevents you from using the ring finger to play.

- This style can be played with or without the use of fingerpicks.

RH Showing Arched Wrist, No Fingers Resting

- If you use this hand position, you will be able to play notes with the ring finger.

- Many players have trouble controlling the other fingers when the ring finger is not anchored.

- This position works best for classical guitarists, who are used to including the ring finger.

positions that are the most efficient ones for executing this style.

RH with Ring Finger Resting near Bridge

- Playing near the bridge produces a brighter tone, which some players like. It is particularly effective if you are playing with other musicians.

- On the other hand, playing near the bridge produces a harsh sound that a solo guitarist might not enjoy.

RH with Ring Finger Resting near Neck

- This produces a more mellow sound.

- It may also be too soft, especially if you are playing with other musicians.

- Try playing in all of these places, and don't feel that you must stay in one place throughout an entire song.

FINGERPICKING

207

THE BASIC STRUM
This is the most basic strum for fingerpicking

Although there are a number of other strums used in finger-picking, this is a good place to start. You will be using the thumb, index, and middle fingers of the right hand. There are four steps:

1) Thumb plays the low bass string.
2) Middle finger picks up on the 1st string.

3) Thumb plays high bass string.
4) Index finger picks up on the 2nd string.

Try playing the notes evenly, four even eighth notes. Later you can start to modify the rhythm by making the first thumb notes just slightly longer than the middle finger notes.

You would be amazed at how many recordings have

Right Thumb Plays Bass Note

- Remember that your tone is very much a function of *where* on the guitar you are picking—at the neck, near the bridge, etc.

- This is a good time to try playing with a thumb pick and fingerpicks.

- After you hit the bass note, the thumb can come to rest on the next string.

RH Middle Finger Picks Up on 3rd String

- Remember that you are picking up, or toward you.

- The middle finger should be curled, and lifted off the string after you play it.

- Don't play too hard. You should hear the note clearly.

been made using this strum. Practice the strum with all of the chords that you have learned so far. Listen to audio track 33 so that you can hear how it sounds. Listen to recordings by John Denver, Joan Baez, or Gordon Lightfoot, all of whom use this strum or variations of it on their recordings. So do many of the excellent country studio players who appear on recordings by most of the country music stars.

Right Thumb Plays Higher Bass Note

- Thumb comes to rest on the next string.

- The thumb will need to move backwards to hit the next low bass note.

- The more specifically you hit the note and avoid other strings, the better it will sound.

Index Finger Picks Up on 2nd String

- This is the last step of the strum.

- Be careful not to hit extraneous strings.

- After you hit the note, your middle finger needs to be prepared to play again when the thumb repeats.

FINGERPICKING

FINGERPICKING IN ACTION
This section will continue to explain the basic fingerpicking strum

Next we will discuss what happens to the fingers after you have hit each of the notes. Before we get into that, let's do a bit of troubleshooting.

Are you:

*   Feeling that your right wrist is tired?
*   Hitting the exact strings that you are aiming at, without extra noises?

*   Playing evenly?

Here are a few playing tips:

*   Keep the right wrist relaxed.
*   Play along with the MP3 (track 33).
*   Don't rush.

Right Thumb after Playing Bass Note

*   Thumb or thumb pick has come to rest on the next string.

*   The thumb should be extended horizontally. Don't bend it excessively

when you do the strum. Excess motion is wasteful.

*   Middle finger should be ready to play the 1st string.

RH Middle Finger after Playing 1st String

*   You should not play the 2nd string. (One string per finger in this strum.)

*   To avoid the 2nd string, curl the finger right after it has hit the 1st string.

*   The right thumb should be in position to play the high bass string.

Try the strum with different chords, playing one complete strum for each chord. For example:

```
T M T I     T M T I     T M T I     T M T I
G           Em          G           D7
```

RH Thumb Playing Higher Bass Note

- Once again, the thumb comes to rest against the next string after playing.

- If you are using a thumb pick, try to minimize the noise of the pick by not playing too hard.

- Some players use a thumb pick, but no fingerpicks. The idea is to make the bass notes stronger.

RH Index Finger Picks Up on 2nd String

- Curl the finger after you hit the note.

- If you use fingerpicks, try to control the pick noise.

- Plastic and metal fingerpicks sound different. Experiment to find the sound you like.

FINGERPICKING

REVERSING THE ORDER
This is essentially the same pick, but the order of the fingers has been reversed

The real fun in fingerpicking comes when you have mastered a half dozen different picking styles, and can mix and match them like a cook at a fine restaurant.

In this strum the order of thumb notes is reversed, with the higher bass note preceding the low one. The index finger will play before the middle finger is put to use. The sequence is:

1) Thumb plays high bass.
2) Index finger plays 2nd string.
3) Thumb plays low bass.
4) Middle finger plays 1st string.

Try it with four even eighth notes, and then try to play

Right Thumb Plays 4th String

- Remember, the thumb is playing the *higher* string first now.

- The thumb can come to rest on the next string, just as it did on the other string; *but* the thumb should be bent back after you play to be ready to play the low bass note.

Right Index Finger Plays 2nd String

- The reverse order of the last strum.

- Curl the finger after you hit the note.

- Thumb should be bent back, ready to play the low bass string.

with the high thumb note lasting just slightly longer than the index finger note. You may find that reversing the order of the notes is mildly disorienting at first, but you should be able to overcome that problem without too much trouble.

As soon as you feel comfortable playing this strum, try alternating between the two picks like this:

```
T M T I   T I T M   T M T I   T I T M   etc.
G           Em
```

Right Thumb Plays 6th String

- Thumb comes to rest on the next string, after playing the string, ready to return to the high bass.

- There is a certain bounce to fingerpicking that the thumb note seems to produce.

- It is possible to mute the notes in fingerpicking, with the palm of the right hand. Chet Atkins often did this in his playing.

Right Middle Finger Plays 1st String

- The sequence will then start again, or you can go back to the first fingerpicking sequence.

- Try playing a bit faster, once you have mastered the strum.

- If you are able to go from one strum to the other, you really understand the notion behind fingerpicking.

213

FINGERPICKING SONGS

Now you can apply fingerpicking to playing songs

In order to make things easy for you, rather than introduce a new song here, we will revisit our old friend the "Crawdad Song," and use the fingerpicking patterns to play it.

- Here is the melody of the "Crawdad Song" again. See if you can mix and match the patterns that I have given you.

214

Sing along: Hurry up babe, you slept too late, honey / Hurry up, babe, you slept too late, babe / Hurry up, babe, you slept too late / The crawdad man has passed your gate / Honey, sugar baby mine.

Sell your crawdads two for a dime, honey / Sell your crawdads two for a dime, babe / Sell your crawdads two for a dime / Your crawdads ain't good as mine / Honey, sugar baby mine.

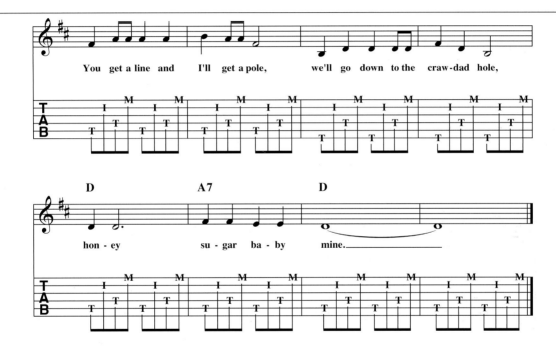

You get a line and I'll get a pole, we'll go down to the craw-dad hole,

D   A7   D

hon-ey   su-gar ba-by   mine.

FINGERPICKING

- Notice that in the first part of the strum, the order is thumb, middle, thumb, index; in the second part the order is thumb, index, thumb, middle.

215

COMBINING THE PATTERNS
We will now combine the two fingerpicking patterns

Combining fingerpicking patterns are what the style is all about. Try the "Crawdad Song" once again, alternating between various picking styles. I haven't given you the finger by finger analysis here; see if you can pick it up from the music or tablature.

Below are a list of fingerpicking patterns for you to try:

Variation 1

1) Thumb plays low bass.
2) Thumb plays high bass while middle finger plays 1st string.
3) Index plays 2nd string.
4) Thumb plays low bass.
5) Middle finger plays 1st string.
6) Thumb plays high bass.
7) Index finger plays 2nd string.

Rhythm: 1 2+ 3+ 4+
Long, short, short, short, short, short, short or quarter note, followed by six eighth notes

Variation 2

1) Thumb plays low bass.
2) Thumb plays high bass.
3) Index finger plays 2nd string.
4) Thumb plays low bass.
5) Middle finger plays 1st string.
6) Thumb plays high bass.
7) Index finger plays 2nd string.

Same rhythm as above, 1 2+ 3+ 4+

Variation 3

1) Thumb plays low bass.
2) Thumb plays high bass while middle finger plays 1st string.
3) Thumb plays low bass.
4) Middle finger plays 1st string.
5) Thumb plays high bass.
6) Index finger plays 2nd string.

Rhythm: Long, long, short, short, short, short
Quarter note, quarter note, four eighth notes

Variation 4

1) Thumb plays low bass.
2) Thumb plays high bass while middlefinger plays 1st string.
3) Thumb plays low bass.
4) Index finger plays 2nd string.
5) Thumb plays high bass.
6) Middle finger plays 1st string.

Rhythm: Long, long, short, short, short, short
Quarter note, quarter note, four eighth notes

The final fingerpicking challenge is to attempt to integrate the ring finger into the strum.
Here's one example:

1) Thumb plays low bass.
2) Thumb plays high bass.
3) Ring finger plays 1st string.
4) Thumb plays low bass string.
5) Index finger plays 3rd string.
6) Middle finger plays 2nd string.

Rhythm: Long, long, short, short, short, short
Quarter note, quarter note, four eighth notes

FINGERPICKING

CHORD DIAGRAMS

CHORDS IN D

D

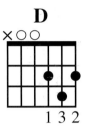

1 3 2

G

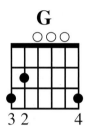

3 2   4

A7

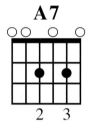

2   3

Bm

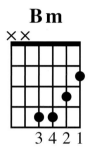

3 4 2 1

Em

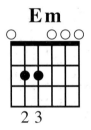

2 3

F♯m

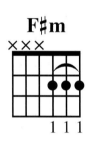

1 1 1

D7

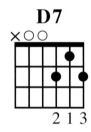

2 1 3

Dmaj7

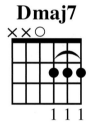

1 1 1

G7

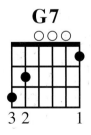

3 2   1

Gmaj7

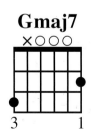

3   1

F

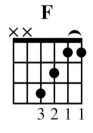

3 2 1 1

Am

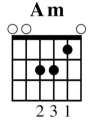

2 3 1

RESOURCES

CHORDS IN G

G
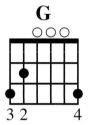

C
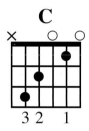

D7
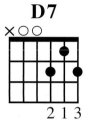

Em
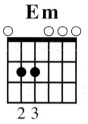

Am
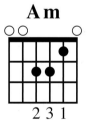

Bm
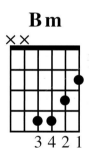

G7
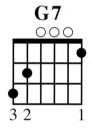

Gmaj7
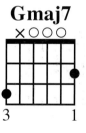

C7
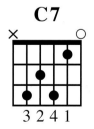

Cmaj7
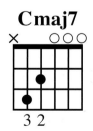

B♭
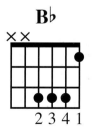

Dm
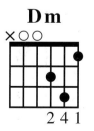

CHORD DIAGRAMS

CHORDS IN C

C

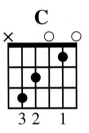

3 2   1

F

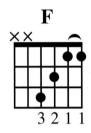

3 2 1 1

G7

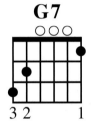

3 2   1

Am

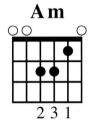

2 3 1

Dm

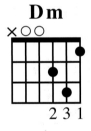

2 3 1

Em

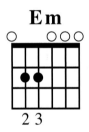

2 3

C7

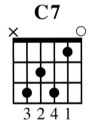

3 2 4 1

Cmaj7

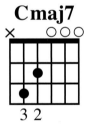

3 2

F7

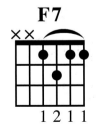

1 2 1 1

Fmaj7

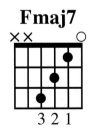

3 2 1

E♭

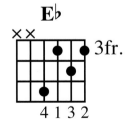

3fr.

4 1 3 2

Gm

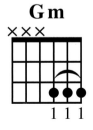

1 1 1

CHORDS IN Em

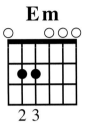

Em

2 3

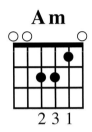

Am

2 3 1

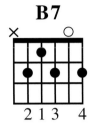

B7

2 1 3   4

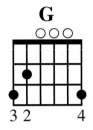

G

3 2   4

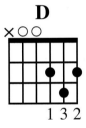

D

1 3 2

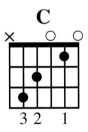

C

3 2   1

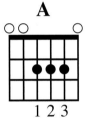

A

1 2 3

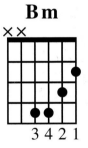

Bm

3 4 2 1

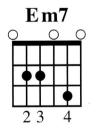

Em7

2 3   4

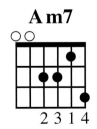

Am7

2 3 1 4

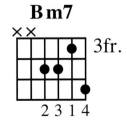

Bm7

3fr.

2 3 1 4

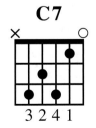

C7

3 2 4 1

CHORD DIAGRAMS

CHORDS IN Am

Am

2 3 1

Dm
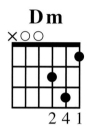
2 4 1

E7
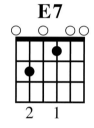
2 1

C
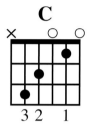
3 2 1

G
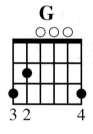
3 2 4

F
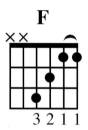
3 2 1 1

C
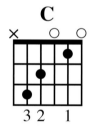
3 2 1

Dm
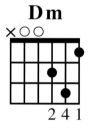
2 4 1

Am7
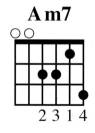
2 3 1 4

Dm7
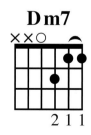
2 1 1

Em7
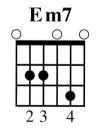
2 3 4

F7
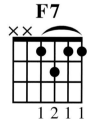
1 2 1 1

CHORDS IN E

E
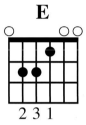

2 3 1

A
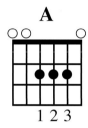

1 2 3

B7
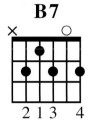

2 1 3 4

C♯m
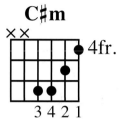

3 4 2 1

F♯m
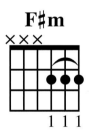

1 1 1

G♯m
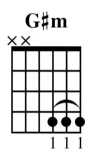

1 1 1

E7
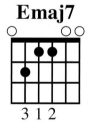

2 1

Emaj7
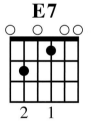

3 1 2

A7
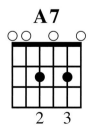

2 3

Amaj7
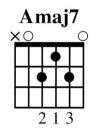

2 1 3

G
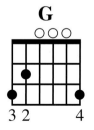

3 2 4

Bm
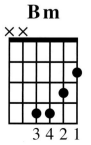

3 4 2 1

SUGGESTED BOOKS & CDS

Below is a short list of useful books about the guitar. There are literally dozens of guitar instruction books available. They cover everything from care and maintenance of the instrument to the history of the instrument, and virtually every possible playing style.

General Works

Coelho, Victor Ananad, ed. *The Cambridge Companion to the Guitar.* Cambridge, UK: Cambridge University Press, 2003

Gerken, Terja, Michael Simmons, Frank Ford, and Richard Johnston. *Acoustic Guitar.* Milwaukee: Hal Leonard Corporation, 2003.

Hunter, Dave. *Acoustic Guitars: The Illustrated Encyclopedia.* San Diego: Thunder Bay Press, 2003.

Rodgers, Jeffrey Pepper. *Beginning Guitarist's Handbook.* San Anselmo, CA: String Letter Publishing, 2001.

Sandberg, Larry. *The Acoustic Guitar Guide, Revised and Updated.* Chicago: Acappella Books, 2000.

Waksman, Steve. *Instruments of Desire: the Electric Guitar and the Shaping of Musical Experience.* Cambridge: Harvard University Press, 1999.

Guitar Instruction

When it comes to actual guitar instruction books, rather than list the hundreds of available books, I will list the names of several authors who turn out consistently reliable instructional materials.

Alternate Tunings and Partial Capos

There are a number of books that cover other tunings for the guitar. I have a book out for Routledge called *Guitar Tunings, A Comprehensive Guide 2006.* Mark Hansen has some good alternate tuning books out as well. Randall Williams, who is a clinician for Kyser capos, has two books out for Hal Leonard that deal with capos and partial capos.

Blues Guitar

Duck Baker and Stefan Grossman are reliable chroniclers of blues guitar styles.

Classical Guitar

Frederick Noad and Aaron Shearer have written a number of books for classical guitar.

The series *Pumping Nylon* by Scott Tennant is very popular. There are also numerous studies by such classical guitar icons as Carcassi and Fernando Sor available.

Jazz

Among the many authors of jazz guitar books, look into the George Van Eps method books, published by Mel Bay. They are difficult books, but excellent for developing advanced techniques. Mel Bay in particular has published numerous jazz guitar guides. Transcriptions of the work of such great jazz players as Barry Galbraith, Pat Martino, and Joe Pass are also available.

World Music

Alfred Music has a series of useful books available that deal with guitar music of Africa, Cuba, Ireland, Spain, etc., and others that adapt the guitar for playing the music of various cultures, such as Japan. My new Mel Bay book, *Non-Jazz Improvisation for Guitar*, includes a number of world music pieces.

Country Guitar
Tommy Flint (published by Mel Bay)
Various transcriptions of such superb country guitarists as Chet Atkins, Norman Blake, Tony Rice, and Doc Watson are useful and inspiring.

Flamenco
Check the Mel Bay catalog for flamenco guitar methods.

Folk Guitar and Fingerpicking
Mark Hansen has a number of excellent books, especially his books on fingerpicking guitar. He has his own company, Accent On Music, which you can find on the Internet at www.accenton music.com

Jerry Silverman has written dozens of books about virtually every aspect of folk guitar.
I have a double CD out with Dan Fox for Music Minus One called *How To Play Folk Guitar*.

225

SUGGESTED VIDEOS & WEB SITES

Videos

Homespun Tapes has many useful guitar instructional videos available, as well as some audio instruction tapes. These include tapes by Happy Traum, Doc Watson, and many other famous artists and instructors.

Web Sites

Check out the following Web sites:

www.accentonmusic.com (Mark Hansen)
www.alfred.com (For Alfred Music)
www.melbay.com
www.halleonard.com
www.HomespunTapes.com

For more information about Dick Weissman and his music, go www.dickweissman.com.

227

GLOSSARY

Acoustic guitar: An unamplified guitar

Acoustic-electric guitar: An acoustic guitar with a pick-up or built in electronics

Action: Height of strings above neck

Amplifier: A stand alone tool that plugs into a wall outlet and into the guitar as well

Arpeggio: Individual series of notes

Arching the hand: Right hand position with strings wrist held upright

Battery-powered amplifier: An amplifier that doesn't require a power source, but runs on batteries

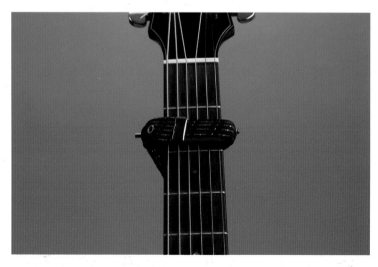

Bracing: Interior guitar supports inside the body of the instrument

Bridge: Each guitar string runs across the bridge into a guitar pin, or in the case of a classical guitar the string is tied by the player

Capo: A tube or clamp that is used to automatically change the key of the guitar

Classical guitar: Nylon string guitar used to play classical music

Dobro: A resonator guitar played flat with a steel bar

End pin: Pin at the end of the guitar that supports a strap

F-hole guitar: A guitar with f holes on the face, instead of a round sound hole. Often used by jazz guitarists

Finger picks: Picks worn on the index, middle and ring fingers of the right hand

Flamenco guitar: A lighter guitar, made of cypress wood, used to play flamenco music

Flat pick: A pick used by guitarists to play rhythm guitar, or individual notes. It is held between the thumb and index fingers of the right hand

Guitar tuner: An electronic tuner that helps the player to tune the guitar to pitch

Hammering On: A technique where notes are actually picked by the left hand

Jazz guitar: Often a hollow-bodied instrument that produces a more mellow sound than the solid body guitar used in rock and roll

Lute: An ancient relative of the guitar, popular at medieval courts of the kings

Nut: The strings run over the nut on the way to the tuning gears

Nylon string guitar: A guitar strung with nylon strings. Used in playing f classical and flamenco guitar music

Partial capo: A capo that covers less than six strings of the guitar

Pick guard: A plastic piece near the guitar sound hole that minimizes the damage from playing hard with picks or fingernails

Requinto: A smaller body guitar, tuned higher than the normal guitar tuning

Rock guitar: Usually a solid body guitar, used in playing rock and roll

Round hole guitar: Guitar with a round sound hole

Slide guitar: A wood- or steel-bodied guitar used in playing Delta blues

Solid body electric guitar: The solid body guitar makes no sound without amplification. It is typically used in rock and roll

Steel string guitar: A guitar that uses steel strings

Thumb pick: A pick worn on the right thumb

Travel guitar: A smaller sized guitar ideal for travelers to bring on airlines

Truss rod: A metal rod placed in the guitar neck to eliminate warping

Tuning gears: The gears that change the pitch of the notes on the guitar

Twelve string guitar: A guitar with six pairs of strings

Ukulele: A cousin of the guitar. It has a smaller body, and originated in Hawaii

Vibrato: A technique used to extend the length of the note by moving fingers up and down a fret repeatedly

Vintage guitar: A highly priced older guitar, sought after by collectors

Warped neck: A guitar neck that is no longer straight, and is therefore difficult or impossible to play

INDEX

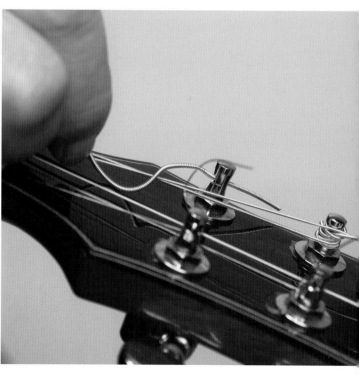